3.50

A.T.T.

from R.H.P.

April 1946

P9-170

Last Mountains

Last Mountains

THE STORY OF THE CASCADES

ROBERT ORMOND CASE AND VICTORIA CASE

DOUBLEDAY, DORAN & CO., INC., GARDEN CITY, N. Y., 1945

Preface

To ATTEMPT to set down impressions of a great mountain range in one volume is to invite the immediate and sometimes sinister interest of three groups of critics.

First is the local citizen, the one-mountain man sworn to defend his adjacent crag against all comers, criticisms, and even comparisons. The suggestion that other peaks also adorn the range arouses his instant suspicion. Failure to apply any adjective less than the superlative to his mountain at once indicates bias. Omission of a single detail from its list of virtues is the ultimate affront.

Scarcely less formidable is the patience with which the historian searches through and disregards the sound wheat of the narrative, grain by grain, until, with a sadistic huzzah, he comes at last to a fragment of chaff which has somehow slipped through the fine-meshed screen. Dr. Marcus Whitman did *not* accompany the Great Migration westward from Fort Hall on October 12, 1843; he had quitted the train three days earlier, eager to outdistance the slow-moving wagons to Whitman's Mission. Sirs, this is an error. The book's tripe.

And the scientist is drawn irresistibly to the precise spot in an otherwise flower-decked and dewy terrain where a toadstool rears its ugly head. Under that toadstool is a single withered leaf, and under the leaf cowers the lone, tiny slug to which our specialist points with horror and distaste. "On page 189," he writes, "third paragraph, line three, occurs the following statement: 'Below the Miocene stratum in the rock structure are many Pleistocene fossils.' The Pleistocene *never* occurs *below* the Miocene. Sirs, the thing stinks."

Nevertheless, aware of the danger of the undertaking, the authors have endeavored to present as accurate and well-balanced a view of the Cascades as space and the limitations of their own enthusiasm permit. Having personally scaled some of the range's major peaks, crossed all its highways, fished most of its famous streams, and traversed its length, both sides, many times, they are conscious of faulty perspective due to perhaps too intimate contact with the magnificent barrier.

For whatever sins of omission or commission which may have crept into the narrative, the reader's indulgence is asked—with the mutual and gracious awareness, it is hoped, that neither the error nor its forgiveness will bring any embarrassment whatever to the mountains themselves. Snow field and austere crest will flame at each succeeding dawn, as usual, massively unconscious of the ill-chosen words or halting phrases of this or any other appraisal. Mountains, somehow, are like that.

THE AUTHORS

Contents

Contents

List of Half-tone Illustrations

Last Mountains

CHAPTER I

The Place Called Oyer-un-gun

THAT JOVIAL CUTTHROAT, Francis Drake, put in somewhere on the Oregon coast in 1579 to take on water and stores, but his quaint log records that the "sunne and starres" were so obscured by a "stinkeing fog" that he was unable to take a bearing. He departed as casually, a few days later, obscured by the same fog; and thus missed the honor of being the first white man to view the Cascade Range—or Cascades—from the sea.

Almost two centuries later, in 1776, Captain James Cook sailed from England, and after exploring the South Pacific, in 1778 put in at Nootka Sound, on the west coast of Vancouver Island, too far north to see the magnificent sweep of the continent's last great barrier. He did, however, take aboard a considerable cargo of near-priceless sea otter pelts; and this was sufficient to lift the region from obscurity.

Many ships quickly converged on the scene, hopeful of tracking down Russia's vast secret supply of sea otter. To the crews of more than one scurvy-ridden trader, beating eastward across the endless swells of the Pacific, the sight of a great silvery dome rearing above the horizon was a welcome one, indeed, and so recorded in their logs. What they saw, long before the green-forested shore appeared, was the crest of Mount Rainier, the highest and most massive peak in the glittering length of the Cascades.

The traders' stories, plus their cargoes of furs, inflamed still other salty explorers. The legend of the mountains and the great "River of the West" grew. Soon came the inevitable clash between expanding empires. Rivals were England, Russia, Spain, and, in the end, that infant prodigy among nations, the United States.

It became, literally, a vast poker game, in which the stakes were the last great unclaimed frontiers of the globe. In the beginning the contestants had no conception of the true dimensions of the prize. It was more than a strip of coast, incalculably more than control of the fur trade. At issue was title to a segment of the earth's surface larger than continental Europe; and California, the entire Southwest, the later acquisition of Alaska—all were contingent purses offered in history's final and most blooded game of chance.

A glance at a modern map gives the geographic setting: the stupendous stage—dominated by the Cascades—upon which the last empire drama unfolded.

Beginning in the brakes of the Fraser River, north of the Canadian border, the continent's longest continuous barrier extends southward six hundred miles to the California line. The general course of the range lies from eighty to a hundred and fifty miles inland, paralleling the coast lines of Oregon and Washington and dividing the two states into halves as effectively as though a giant wall had been reared for the purpose.

It is almost a literal wall, being broken at but one point,

near its middle, where the Columbia has cut a neat and formidable gorge westward to the sea. Except for this break,
the giant ridge averages a mile high throughout its length;
and from that massive sky line ten individual peaks soar beyond the 10,000-foot level.[1] Each stands alone, each within
view of its neighbor in a stately procession that dips below
the curves of the horizon.

The sentinel peaks dominated the lives and legends of the
local Indians, just as they affect the destinies of those living
today on the Pacific slope. The range as a whole comprises
one of the continent's most magnificent panoramas, visible
for many miles from the east and far out to sea.

Few of the interior Indians ever crossed the ridge in ages
past. The easiest route was through the Columbia gorge,
and that was ominous enough. It was walled in by cliffs that
were almost vertical and, at some points, thousands of feet
high. On foot it was a man-killing haul; and formidable
rapids, or "cascades"—for which the range was later named
—held back all but the most skilled boatmen.

Painted warriors of the high desert often dreamed of the
ever-green land west of The Mountains. It was said to be a
mild and exceedingly pleasant region, prosperous and well
watered. Game, fish, and fruit were abundant there. Extremes of summer heat or winter cold were alike unknown,
and storms never blew. The wistful Shoshone word for the
nameless region was Oyer-un-gun,[2] or "Place of Plenty."

[1]Including Mount St. Helens, claimed among the "major peaks," although its actual height, as given by the United States Coast and Geodetic
Survey, is 9671 feet.

[2]One of the many disputed origins of the word "Oregon." Others include the Spanish *Aura Agua*—"Gently Falling Water," and the Algon-
quin *Wau-re-gan*—"Beautiful Water."

CHAPTER II

Marked Cards

THE CONTEST to gain this final empire was not a gentlemanly one. As in all international maneuvering, no ethical scruples entered. Moreover, the race was not necessarily to the swift and strong. First to discover this was Captain George Vancouver, of His Majesty's Navy.

Vancouver arrived in North Pacific waters in 1792, in command of three British ships flying the red and blue of the British Merchant Marine. They were armed, manned, and provisioned for a two-year cruise. Vancouver had three different chores to do, each a delight to his buccaneer heart.

The first was to find out if there was, actually, a great "River of the West" flowing into these waters. If so, explore it, and formally claim it for the Crown. Next, proceed northward to Nootka Sound, chart all geographical features en route, name them, and claim them for the Crown. Finally, armed with these claims, put in at Nootka Sound for a conference with a representative of Spain, one Bodega y Cuadra. The purpose of this conference: to decide who owned all of the continent bordering on the North Pacific.

Vancouver was not worried about the tilt with Cuadra. It

would be a diplomatic farce, diverting but meaningless. Spain's claims rested largely upon an ancient and decrepit papal decree giving her title to all shores washed by the waters of the Pacific Ocean. Britain was no longer overawed by Rome. Those formidable sea hawks—Drake, Hawkins, and Frobisher—had taken the measure of Spain more than a century before.

Russia was the only unknown equation. Russian sealers were encroaching farther southward each season, extending trails blazed by Vitus Bering and his roaring crew. St. Petersburg was still trying to make something of the Bering business, but that trusty formula, "rights of discovery," plus England's growing sea power, would soon dispel such foggy pretenses.

Thus Vancouver, believing himself to be plowing through what were practically British waters, was astonished and annoyed when he met the sturdy sloop *Columbia*, commanded by Captain Robert Gray, of Boston, beating southward at a leisurely pace. What chance, or sinister design, had brought this brash Yankee skipper more than fourteen thousand miles from his home port?

They hailed each other, hove to, and Gray came aboard. Vancouver's chagrin soon merged into an amused relief. The forthright Gray was completely friendly. His was a private venture, backed by Boston merchants. He was interested only in the fur of the sea otter. He thought he'd found the entrance to a great river, and wondered if the natives upstream might know these valuable furs. He'd stood offshore for nine days waiting for a favorable wind. Now he was on his way south to try again. He seemed only dimly aware, if at all, of the shadow of international events.

Vancouver was elated. "Let him waste his time off that bay," he told his lieutenant, Broughton, when they left Gray behind. "He'll find no river. Three years hence he'll be paying tribute to England for any furs he gathers here."

Vancouver continued up the coast, sighted and named Mount Rainier and Mount Baker, explored and named Vancouver Island, Puget Sound, and numerous other islands and inlets. It was a good summer's business for the empire. Then he put in at the rendezvous at Nootka Sound.

In the midst of the session with Cuadra—which was as diverting as Vancouver had anticipated, warmed by much Barbados rum—the sloop *Columbia* yawed casually into the sound and dropped anchor. The merrymakers saw him from Cuadra's "fort," a log-walled structure pretending to symbolize Spain's dominance of the region. They raised another glass in mock sympathy for the unlettered Yankee trader who had blundered so far from his familiar shores.

But Broughton came hurriedly and whispered in his superior's ear. Vancouver paled. "Impossible, Broughton! The man's mad."

"I doubt it, sir. He has charts."

"Have him and his charts aboard at once," Vancouver directed.

Breaking off his mummery with Cuadra on some pretext, Vancouver hurried down to his flagship. Gray was waiting, his broad, weather-beaten face alight. He could scarcely wait until the rum was poured before repeating his news. He had discovered the "River of the West." From its volume it was one of the mightiest on the continent. It entered the Pacific just south of Cape Disappointment, where both Vancouver and his predecessor Meares had declared there was no river.

"Nonsense," said Vancouver smilingly. But his blood ran cold. Instinctively he jockeyed for position. "We saw that bay, of course. So did Meares. That's no discovery, sir."

"But did you cross the bar?" Gray demanded, beaming. "Did you find it wasn't a bay but a river? Did Meares?"

"Did you?" Vancouver countered.

"We did." Gray spread his charts on the table. "Look—here are the soundings. It shoals at the bar—three fathoms, ye'll note. Now you're riding deep and free, in fresh water. We filled our casks."

"Fresh water?" said Vancouver, his lips thin.

"The best. Come aboard and have a swig of it." Gray's boastfulness was entirely friendly. He spoke as one salty explorer to another, eager for commendation. "It's a mighty river, Captain. We've named it the Columbia. . . . We put ashore here for trade. It's black with savages. They're thunderstruck at the ship—they've never seen anything like it. And, man, what trade! Four otter skins for a sheet of copper. Beaver skins two spikes each. Other land furs one spike each. There's fifty villages up above, the savages say. . . ."

He babbled exultantly on, unaware how bitter was the torture he was inflicting on his listener. He told how he had sailed upstream until the water shoaled, found and charted the main channel, and then had gone ashore with his mate, Boit, and claimed the river and all it drained on behalf of the United States. . . . Gray was a little shamefaced at this detail. It smacked of pomp and circumstance repugnant to the ideals of the youthful republic.

"I don't hold much truck with that gibberish," he admitted. "Even those naked heathens thought it funny—waving a rusty cutlass like that, and muttering. But I reckoned it had to be done, so we did it fit and proper. What matters is, we found her. The river's the thing, and she's ours! We've named her the Columbia. . . ."

Vancouver studied the chart. Truth was written there. It was self-evident. He remembered now the muddy current that moved his ship as he stood offshore. There'd been trees floating in it too. How had he been so blind as to judge that outflow anything else than a mighty river? His thoughts fled to far-off London. What would the Admiralty have to say—yes, and Downing Street—about this debacle? What was the empty honor of naming the peaks, if title to the land itself was in dispute? Gray had claimed the river and *all it drained*.

He became aware, incredulously, of what Gray was saying.

"You'll want to take a look at it on your way south. So copy the charts tonight." Gray indicated his records with a horny forefinger. "I'll pick these up in the morning."

Vancouver glanced up at him, then quickly pretended to study the chart. It was to hide the sudden, inner flame of exultation. "Do you mean it, sir?"

"Why not?" said Gray affably. "I'm loaded. You're not trading. Sure, copy it. You'll need those soundings if you go inside."

"Thank you," said Vancouver. He glanced once at Broughton, who had been a silent, perspiring spectator, and back at Gray. "Where do you sail from here?"

"North for a piece. Just to see what the coast looks like. There's plenty of time. When it's winter here is when I catch the best winds at the Horn."

Vancouver nodded. It was perfect. He would arrive in London months before Gray made it to Boston. "Thank you," he repeated. "You'll have the charts back in the morning, Captain."

Thirty days later Vancouver anchored off the mouth of the Columbia. He deemed the bar too dangerous for his largest ship, the *Discovery*, but the brig *Chatham*, commanded by Broughton, went in boldly, following Gray's charts. He reported to Vancouver that it was, in fact, a huge river. Vancouver ordered him to explore it further, and himself hurried south to Monterey to prepare for the long haul home.

Broughton sailed a hundred and twenty-five miles upriver, staggered by each succeeding vista. The countryside was green and well watered, clothed with such timber as neither he nor his crew had ever before seen. The mountains grew closer. He named two of the shining peaks: Mount Hood and Mount St. Helens. They were rooted in a towering range that completely walled off the east.

Just short of the gorge, Broughton was halted by cascades in the river. He turned back, knowing he had glimpsed an inland empire. It was absolutely untouched, unknown. Time was of the essence now. Where was Gray?

Gray, still cruising comfortably in the north, was left far behind. When Broughton reported in London he made no mention of Gray's charts. He asserted that Gray had merely anchored in a bay and was unaware of the existence of the river.

Britain not only laid claim to the river by right of discovery; she followed the idea conveniently suggested by Gray and claimed all lands drained by the great waterway and all its branches.

CHAPTER III

Pattern of Destiny

From their lofty grandstand seats during the next decades the mountains must have smiled, many times, at the puny antics and wranglings that followed rival claims of "discovery." Though the river and the seasons contrived to roll on as usual, the quiet of the centuries was disturbed by insect shouts about "rights" and "title" and dire threats of war.

The dispute was called the "Oregon Question"; and it took many bizarre twists during its half-century course. In the end, and step by step at crucial points, it was chance, not ruthless scheming, that decided the issue.

Spain was soon outbluffed by England, according to schedule. Russia cautiously withdrew to the Bering and consolidated there. This left England facing the infant United States, and the next step was obvious. The world's most powerful and battle-scarred empire builder was prepared to follow the usual formula: move in while the dispute raged, establish a "protective" stewardship—and back up the new status quo, which was physical possession, with men-of-war.

But chance brought a young Corsican named Bonaparte

out of obscurity and made him master of Europe. For a time Britain was engaged in the business of survival. When a breathing spell came, and the opportunity to look over the global picture, Downing Street found to its indignation that the brash Yankees had stolen a leaf from their own book of empire strategy. Not only had they "purchased" the entire Mississippi River and its branches from Napoleon, which gave them title to most of the continent, but they had sent the Lewis and Clark Expedition overland to thread the Columbia gorge and resurvey the river to the sea. Worse still, a New York merchant, John Jacob Astor, had founded a trading post called Astoria at the mouth of the Columbia.

The War of 1812 was Britain's round. In what American historians rate as a successful war, the American flag disappeared from the seven seas. Thus a British gunboat dropped in unopposed at Astoria. When it departed the Northwest Fur Company, a British concern, occupied Astor's late fort. The transaction was called a sale, but it developed later that Astor's trusted employees, who had negotiated the sale, had been British citizens all the while.

Out of that episode came the Joint Occupation Treaty of 1818, which was considered very satisfactory to Downing Street. Any entering wedge was sufficient. The Northwest Fur Company was soon swallowed up by that expanding giant, the Hudson's Bay Company. Headquarters were quietly moved upriver to Fort Vancouver, just above the junction of the Willamette River with the Columbia River, west of the Cascades. Southward lay the immense Willamette Valley; the mountains lay immediately to the east. Extending north to Puget Sound was an equally rich country.

Placed in charge at Fort Vancouver was Dr. John Mc-Loughlin, destined to become one of the region's immortals. He was a stern yet kindly man, thoroughly versed in global strategy. He was under specific orders to discourage settlement of the land and to preserve and consolidate the area for Britain.

On the face of it this made Britain's position secure. The British flag now flew above Fort Vancouver. Though settlement of the land was only "discouraged," not backed by force, the effect was the same, since the Hudson's Bay Company controlled the sole source of supplies and equipment. It was believed that all settlement must come from the sea, since the American frontier was still on the Missouri, half a continent distant. By the time that frontier crept westward —it might take two centuries—Britain's interests would need no further "protection."

This time-tested theory ran foul of a pattern of destiny seemingly higher than the laws of chance or the schemes of empire builders. Often enough, during the preceding eight centuries, Britain had profited by the "unpredictable grain of sand." This time the scales tipped against her.

The Indians east of the Cascades must find their living on the dry, barren plateaus. The exigencies of their life made them active, warlike, and shrewd. They were also impoverished, perpetually in search of new sources of food. Observing the well-fed white men—trappers, voyageurs, and explorers—come and go in what appeared to be an inexhaustible wealth, they decided the white man's gods must be more powerful than their own, brewers of stronger "medicine." Inquiry revealed that there was a Book telling all.

They sent several of their braves on the long trip to St. Louis to get a copy of the Book and bring it back.

Though it appears that the not-too-simple red man was more concerned with his material than spiritual poverty, his request for the Book was taken as a cry for salvation. Church groups were immediately enthused, with the result that several young missionaries were commissioned to carry the Word into the wilderness.

One of these was the Rev. Jason Lee, who crossed the plains and went down the Columbia in 1834. He was welcomed at Fort Vancouver by McLoughlin, who persuaded Lee and his party to settle in the Willamette Valley within visiting distance of the fort, rather than returning east of the Cascades. Like all despots, McLoughlin was a lonely man. The missionaries seemed harmless enough. What were so few among so many?

But Lee's letters to his superiors back in St. Louis, widely circulated, described the vast and fertile Willamette Valley, and the mild, year-round climate sheltered by the Last Mountains. "No cyclones here," Lee reported tersely. "No crop failures. No zero weather. No Indian trouble." Spreading like wildfire throughout Missouri and eastward, this became the more poetic "land where flowers bloom at Christmas and storms never blow" and the state of mind engendered by these descriptions became known as the "Oregon fever."

It was a small seed planted along the westward-looking frontier. From it grew that phenomenon among nomadic movements: the covered-wagon emigration.

One practical detail at first barred the way of the covered

wagons: how cross the two thousand-odd exceedingly hostile miles stretching from Missouri to the free land "out yonder"? This was answered by Dr. Marcus Whitman and his beautiful wife, Narcissa, who followed Lee and established a mission east of the Cascades—where they were to fall victim, eleven years later, to the weapons of the disillusioned and still famine-stricken Indians of the high plateau. Whitman, a tough-fibered man, brought a wagon across the continent in the face of continual assertions en route that it couldn't be done. Although he was forced to dismember the wagon at the Snake River, major eastward tributary of the Columbia, a trail lay behind him from the Missouri to a point well beyond the Rockies.

Along the trail, in 1842, crept a few venturesome families. Close to a hundred were in the party the following year. All were fed and rejuvenated at Whitman's Mission, which was short of the Cascades. After threading the Columbia gorge, the emigrants were welcomed by the now well-established Jason Lee mission in the Willamette Valley. Even Dr. McLoughlin, kindly of heart, unaware as yet that these impoverished pilgrims represented the first trickles of an impending flood, was incapable of denying the necessities of life to the newcomers.

The next year, 1843, the flood broke. At old Independence, on the west bank of the Missouri near the present site of Kansas City, nine hundred men, women, and children assembled their wagons and lashed on all their worldly possessions. It was the Great Migration of '43. Whitman, returning from a journey to Washington, was on hand to lead them westward; and history's most colorful mass migration got under way.

Simultaneously, out on the banks of the Willamette, unknown to the leaders of the Great Migration, came one of the inscrutably timed gestures of free men. A handful of settlers gathered at a place called Champoeg to set up a "provisional government." McLoughlin rushed all his available trappers and traders to the spot, intending to dominate the meeting. The vote was close. When the tally was counted it was found that by the weight of two votes—51 to 49—the Oregon Provisional Government had been established under the American flag.

It was a narrow but sufficient margin. The arrival of the Great Migration that fall gave a predominance to the American settlers that could not again be challenged. The next year 1500 more arrived, swarming down through the Columbia gorge like trail-weary but triumphant barbarians descending on Rome. A tide was under way that was to ebb and flow, but continue unchecked through the following century.

The Champoeg incident caught Britain unawares. She had been trapped by her own shrewdly established premise: that occupancy, peaceful penetration, settlement must be the sole determining factor in solving the Oregon Question. As a final gesture, for trading purposes, she claimed everything north of the Columbia River. The question was finally compromised, with the forty-ninth parallel extending westward from the Rockies to the coast; then the international boundary line curved to follow the channel around the southern tip of Vancouver Island.

Thus the winner—the United States—gathered in the winnings in this giant poker game. She had a foothold on the Pacific; and that was sufficient. Two years later the Stars and Stripes waved in California. Settlement of the Mexican War brought in the Southwest; and the task of consolidating and developing the continent from coast to coast—the richest single segment of the earth's surface—was under way.

Mr. Duniway's mother, Mrs. Abigail Scott Duniway was a member of the above group.

CHAPTER IV

Coming of the Wagons

INDIANS on the Pacific side of the Cascades believed that great spirits—brewers of incomparably powerful "medicine"—lived in the towering peaks. Somewhere above the mile-high timber line, above lifeless lava and the desolate snow fields, in the howling crags where thin tides of space thrummed forever and no man of flesh and blood had ever set foot, these imaginative deities were enthroned. They ruled cloud and storm. The wind blew and the rain fell at their command. Creators of the ever-green land stretching westward to the sea, on their benevolent whim all life depended.

In no other way could tribal philosophers and legend makers explain what is today one of the geophysical marvels of the hemisphere: the manner in which the Cascades not only separate two worlds, but completely dominate the climate, flora, and fauna of the Pacific slope.

East of the great barrier is a high, dry plateau region characterized by extremes of temperature, light rainfall, and "sagebrush and sand" agriculture. Much of it is waste land, known to early chroniclers as the Oregon high desert. Winters are bitter there. In midsummer heat mirages shimmer in the waterless lake beds and dust pillars support the brazen sky.

The Pacific slope, across the Cascades, could easily be on another planet. Within fifty miles—or less than thirty via the Columbia gorge, the main east-west gateway—the traveler emerges abruptly upon a mild, well-watered, perpetually green world. The hills are heavily timbered. Myriad streams born of melting snows flow westward, each bordered by its fertile valley. It is obvious from the luxuriant vegetation and the variety of crops that extremes of heat and cold are unknown in this region.

This striking difference in climate is due to the protective wall of the Cascades, which shuts off both the winter storms and the summer heat of the eastern plateau. The moist winter winds, wheeling in along a great arc from the Aleutians, tempered by the warmth of the Japan Current, are likewise held in and deflected southward by the great barrier. Some of the results of this meteorological phenomenon verge on the incredible.

In the Puget Sound area, for example, at a latitude corresponding to that of Newfoundland, there are grown men who have never seen zero weather, nor slept a summer night through without blankets. They have never seen a tornado or severe electrical storm. North Powder, Oregon, on the eastern plateau, is the coldest spot on the Union Pacific Railroad. At Portland, west of the barrier, roses are picked from the garden on Christmas Day, and golfers, more often than not, play their New Year's round in shirt sleeves.

The luxuriant vegetation of the region is not due to ex-

THE CASCADES SENTINEL PEAKS
Looking south from 11,000-foot crest of Mount Hood

Ray Atkeson

THE COLUMBIA GORGE

cessive rainfall, as is popularly supposed,[1] but to the enormous quantities of snow deposited along the timbered crest of the Cascades each winter when the moisture-laden winds from the Pacific collide, head on, with the chill of the high desert. It is the heaviest snowfall of the continent. Billions of tons of water are thus held in natural storage, melting slowly during the long summer and seeping down through the timbered hills and valleys on its return to the sea.

With the exception of the Columbia, which springs from the foothills of the Canadian Rockies, all rivers entering the Pacific from California to Puget Sound are rooted in the Cascades and coastal hills. This includes the Willamette River, wholly contained in Oregon, whose flow is larger than that of the Missouri, and whose valley, two hundred miles long and from forty to sixty miles wide, was the "Place of Plenty" of Shoshone legend.

The valley was also the free land "over yonder" whose promise caused hardy souls in Missouri and eastward to forsake their familiar, secure environment, gather up all their worldly possessions, and embark upon history's longest and most formidable emigrant trail.

The gods of the mountains must have chuckled when they saw the wagons coming, particularly those jovial sprites presumed to be enthroned on the "guardian peaks"— Mounts Hood, Adams, and St. Helens—above the Columbia gorge. The millenniums had never seen a more nondescript army approach the barrier.

Its arrival was unimpressive. First there was a thin banner of dust that wavered along the sweltering eastward horizon.

[1]The annual precipitation at Portland and Seattle is almost identical with that of New York City.

It grew with the hours. Then tiny horsemen appeared there, in dim silhouette, their long rifles sloping. Behind them the wagons emerged, one by one, forming a long line which crawled with incredible slowness, like a chain of weary and heavily burdened insects. The sway-backed tops of the "prairie schooners" were patched and weather-beaten. Greaseless axles squealed down the jolting column. Only the mothers with babes rode the wagons; the others plodded with the oxen, the weaker women and children clinging to the endgates. At the rear came the loose stock, driven by the single men and boys.

By no outward clue could such a trail-battered crew be recognized as a conquering horde. Yet this was history's Great Migration of '43, and in it was a different breed of men than had previously viewed the Cascades. Others had come and gone. These, bringing their women, children, and farm gear with them, were here to stay. Their descendants, and those who followed along a trail that now stretched an unbroken eighteen hundred miles to old Independence, were destined to hew the forests, till the land, build roads, schools, and great cities. They were to conquer the Columbia gorge and accomplish that which the mountains had failed to do: dam the mighty Columbia itself.

And when they scaled the topmost crags of the highest peaks they even had the last laugh: they found the thrones empty, the pagan gods gone.

Leaders of the '43 trains knew that their most severe test awaited them at the "last mountains." Had they had doubts on this point in the beginning, the stories told by trappers and traders at the wilderness posts would have prepared them. At Forts Laramie and Bridger, and finally at Fort

Hall, the gateway to the "Oregon country" where the sardonic mountain men had gathered to watch the wagons pass, the emigrants were spared no ominous detail concerning the Cascades and the Columbia gorge.

In the first place, they were told, the wagons would never reach the barrier because of a great waterless desert awaiting beyond the Snake River. The Snake itself could not be followed, since it described a great arc northward and threaded a gorge of its own that was more than a mile deep.[2] To attempt to cross the desert cutoff would mean stark tragedy. Horsemen could make it, but the bleached bones of the women, children, and oxen would whiten the plateau.

In the second place, should they make it to the mountains through some miracle, they would find the barrier impassable except at the gorge; and no wagon had ever, nor would ever, thread that cleft. They pictured vast cataracts there, rolling and thundering at the base of towering cliffs. A few canoes had made it downstream, by hugging the shore line, portaging, putting forth cautiously again; but where could even this dangerous transportation be found for such a company, assuming that all the wagons and all the gear were left behind?

And finally, what awaited on the other side? It was no rainbow's end, the mountain men asserted; no Promised Land. On the contrary, it was a dark and dripping wilderness, covered with timber two hundred feet high. This gloomy forest was broken only by countless roaring rapids and canyons that "stood on end." Sole inhabitants were timber wolves, a few hardy trappers, and a scattering of

[2]This detail among the "tall tales" of the Fort Hall traders was a fact. Certain portions of the Snake River gorge are deeper than the Grand Canyon.

fish-eating, vermin-infested Indians who eked out a miserable existence along the rain-swept ocean shore.

The hardheaded emigrants were somewhat armored against such attacks, being no mean storytellers themselves. Also, the motives back of these discouraging tales were plain. The mountain men professed to scorn agriculture, yet secretly feared the coming of the wagons. It meant permanent settlement of the land, which meant the end of the fur trade. The British factor at Fort Hall had his own ax to grind: to turn back the wagons, if possible, and thus protect the interests of the Hudson's Bay Company—and of the empire—west of the Cascades.[3]

Moreover, the emigrants were fortunate in having with them Dr. Marcus Whitman himself, the first to bring a wagon west to Fort Hall. Whitman's Mission was short of the Cascades, and the famous missionary purposed to quit them there. Nevertheless, Whitman had personally threaded the Columbia gorge, down to Fort Vancouver and return, and his calm assurance that the gorge was "dangerous but passable"—by raft or boat—was all that the confident pioneers needed. They had already crossed half a continent. They had forded the Platte River many times, and the formidable Green. They could build boats and rafts, if necessary.

In spite of Whitman's assurance and their own self-reliance, more than one stout heart quailed when the final test came: when the "high desert" was safely past, Whitman had given them Godspeed at the mission and they faced toward the mountains alone.

[3] It is not clear whether the Hudson's Bay factor, Grant, knew at that time—October 1843—of the Champoeg incident, previously described, which had occurred five months before.

CHAPTER V

The Columbia Gorge

THREE THINGS staggered the leaders of the train when they approached the barrier, prepared though they had been by Whitman and others, plus their own trail experience. They found that the Cascades were literally impassable except at the gorge—something they had secretly disbelieved, having seen many mountains. The river was far huger and more imposing than they had imagined. Lastly, approach to the gorge itself was deceptive; it bared its teeth gradually. The treeless hills rose imperceptibly higher. The low banks became walls that crept skyward at each succeeding bend. The green of timber appeared in the heights. Cliffs towered blackly in the distance, downstream, and the river seemed to take a sharp bend, so that only farther walls were visible. Still, they had seen worse trails, rough as the going was at the water's edge.

Thus it was with a feeling of profound shock that the mounted leaders of the train came within view of the first rapids and saw the sunlight flashing on the farther "dalles" —the name given by earlier voyagers to the long stretch of turbulent water caused by hidden obstacles far under the speeding current. It seemed incredible that the great river could be contained in so narrow a space. The surroundings themselves were forbidding. Though this point could be passed by the wagons, the bared teeth of the gorge were beginning to show.

Jesse Applegate, one of the leaders of the '43 train, attempted to set down his impressions of this stretch, his awe plainly tinged with the hard-bitten humor typical of his breed:

> At this place the banks of the river approach within a few yards of each other, and are faced with overhanging cliffs of volcanic stone as black as pot metal, and the channel is not only narrow but crooked also, making this part of the river dangerous to navigation by boats or canoes. I cannot describe the picture I have in mind of that part of the river except to say it must have looked like the place the old Hebrew Elohim fixed his eye upon when "his wrath waxed hot and he said Anathema Marantha."

Under the circumstances, this was mild language indeed, considering the pioneers' gift for blunt speech. What some of Applegate's short-tempered followers said when they appraised these final hazards is unrecorded. A few were undoubtedly dismayed; others, as certainly, hid their apprehension under lurid profanity and voted to get on with it— come to grips with whatever lay ahead. These were the driving spirits of the train, the true trail blazers.

Imaginative writers have clothed the emigrants with incredible virtues. The men were invariably bearded Lincolns, roughhewn and uncompromising. The accumulated sadness of the ages peered from beneath the poke bonnets of the women. Even the children were touched with a species of exalted melancholy: apprentice martyrs, as it were, awaiting sacrifice on the altar of destiny.

Fortunately no such breed existed. As contemporary diaries reveal, attested by living men whose grandfathers crossed the plains and threaded the gorge, the '43 emigrants were an entirely normal and "folksy" crew: hardy, adventurous, accustomed to primitive surroundings. Their forefathers had crossed the Alleghenies and penetrated to the Missouri frontier. They in turn yielded to the urge to move westward. Many of the hardships of the trail were no greater than those accepted as day-by-day routine in old Missouri.

To compensate for these hardships there had been many beautiful days and nights on the plains. The men had hunted, and enjoyed it. The women were surrounded by old neighbors and friends. Each day, for the children, had been a new and thrilling adventure. They had gone hungry at times; they had also feasted often. By night, within the secure circle of the wagons, there had been much singing, shouting, and telling of tall stories. Courtships had ripened as they marched. There had been marriages and births. When the weak and aged died they had buried them, wept, and moved on.

No crusading zeal inspired this westward march. Hardheaded, hard-working men—often tobacco-chewing, swearing men—simply wanted a square mile of that rich, free land in the Oregon country. To achieve it meant security in their old age; they would "do better by the children." It was entirely incidental to that achievement—they were unaware of any such notion, in fact—that they had gained and tamed an empire.

The '43 train wasted no time meeting the challenge of the gorge. There was no time to be lost. Summer had long since waned. Winters were said to be mild beyond the gorge, but the bite of frost was already in the air of mornings on the high desert side.

They laboriously surmounted the high promontory above the rapids and thus gained a new perspective of the great cleft downriver. Rain was slanting there, but through it could be seen sheer cliffs rising up from the current, their crests merging into the clouds. They descended their last hill, crept for miles along the rocky terrain that bordered the speeding current, and so came to the gateway village of The Dalles, nestling on the last flat short of the gap.

Here, for the wagons, ended the transcontinental haul. Many eyes misted as the travel-worn vehicles were abandoned, sold to the traders or their sound running gear dismantled and loaded on the rafts. It was like breaking up a home that had provided shelter from many a storm. Yet it had to be done. Nothing on wheels had penetrated farther west.

The '43 emigrants fared well on this last ominous lap. McLoughlin had sent up boats and skilled voyageurs to meet the train, with orders to take aboard the "sick and destitute" and see them safely through. Thus only the able-bodied were left behind. These built rafts or whipsawed lumber for more manageable boats, and pushed off singly and by twos and threes into the outspread arms of the formidable gorge.

Succeeding trains were not so fortunate. McLoughlin could not long afford to take care of the swelling tide of emigrants. Land speculators and locators took over, offering boat space at prohibitive prices. Unable to pay in cash, and with nothing to barter, more than one destitute family head felled trees at the river's edge, built a raft of logs roped precariously together, loaded on all his possessions, and put forth into the grip of the current.

The threading of the gorge was an epic in itself. The passage not only bristled with danger but was close to the ultimate in sheer discomfort. Winter was always breathing on the backs of these unfortunates, and the cold of the high desert, pouring down through the cleft and meeting the moist warmth of the valley head on, produced the foulest weather of the year. It required many days for an amateur to run the fifty-mile gantlet, because of the portages and the necessity of minute-by-minute vigilance in the speeding current.

One of these assaults on the last barrier—typical of unrecorded scores and hundreds—is described in the diary of Mrs. Cornelius Smith, formerly Elizabeth Dixon, who reached The Dalles with her husband and seven children on October 27, 1847, having been continuously on the trail from La Porte, Indiana, since April 12.

What makes Mrs. Smith's record impressive are the details she fails to mention. She was too close to the water, to danger, starvation, and death, to take note of the awesome environment through which they moved. The towering walls were remote; she had eyes only for her children, her precious household belongings, and the minute-by-minute struggle for survival. The party took longer than ordinary—twenty-six days—to achieve the threshold to the valley. Only once did a hint of desperation creep into the narrative. Not once did she mention any doubt but that they would finally make it through.

CHAPTER VI

Elizabeth Smith—Trail Blazer

"Here are a great many immigrants in camp," Mrs. Smith writes, of their arrival in The Dalles, "some making rafts, others going down in boats which have been sent up by the speculators."

Having no money for the speculators, the Smiths joined with Adam Polk and Russell Welch and their families, and hurried to the business of building a raft. Winter was coming on in the high country. The wind was blowing colder each night.

October 29 was rainy and cold. "The men are making rafts, women cooking and washing, children crying. Indians are bartering potatoes for shirts. They must have a good shirt for half a peck of potatoes."

The next day: "Snow is close by. We should have gone over the mountains [via the Barlow Trail, just opened and still close to impassable] but they are covered with snow, consequently we must go down by water." This typically matter-of-fact statement gives no hint of the forebodings which must have gripped her as she looked at the gorge, the snow-covered mountains, and the darkening sky. If she had fears of the rapids or the raft she hid them, though her seven children ranged from a sixteen-year-old, a boy, down to a babe in arms.

The wind was blowing gusty and strong. They waited in vain throughout the next precious day for a favorable moment to embark. The next day, November 2, they pushed off into the current. "We took off our wagon wheels, laid them on the raft, placed the wagon bed on them, and started, three families of us, on twelve logs, eighteen inches through and forty feet long. The water runs three inches on our raft."

They made only a few miles in the cold weather. The wind was now howling through the gorge. They pulled up at the river's edge, waiting for the water to become calmer. It being impossible to sleep on the raft, they "clambered up a side hill among the rocks and built a fire to cook and warm ourselves and children, while the wind blew and the waves rolled beneath."

Each day following they put out and slid down a few miles and tied up again, the water becoming rougher and colder. Polk became sick, leaving only her husband, Smith, and their oldest boy to manage the 40-foot raft. Welch and the younger Smith boys, meanwhile, were driving the oxen over an exceedingly rough cattle trail which paralleled the river above the 2000-foot southern wall. This trail descended to the river about halfway through the gorge. The oxen would be brought down at this point to help portage the wagons and equipment around the impassable "cascades," the final rapids short of the threshold.

Around November 8 the party's provisions ran low. Polk was dying. Welch was still battling to bring the oxen through, far up in the snow-drifted heights. This meant that Smith must go off on foot along the bank to find an emigrant party or Indians from whom food might be secured. The sixteen-year-old Smith boy was left in charge of the raft.

While her husband was gone, Mrs. Smith wrote simply: "The waves are dashing over the raft, and icicles hanging from the wagon beds to the water. Tonight, at dusk, Adam Polk expired. No one with him but his wife and myself. We sat up all night with him while the waves were dashing below."

Two days later Smith returned, bringing fifty pounds of beef. Once more they ventured forth, but the wind forced them back to shore. "Husband and boy were an hour and a half after dark getting the raft landed and all made fast, while the water ran knee-deep over the raft and the wind blew freezing cold. We women and children did not attempt to get out of our wagons tonight." Meanwhile Polk lay in his wagon, awaiting burial.

The next day, November 11, they made three miles downriver, and "found Welch and the boys waiting with the cattle, which could be driven no farther on this side of the river. Here is a ferry for the purpose of ferrying immigrant cattle across the river."

They buried Polk on the north bank of the river. Two days were spent ferrying the animals across. Finally "we got the ferry man to shift our load to their boat and take us down to the falls [the upper end of the cascades] where we found quite a town of people waiting for their cattle to pull them around the portage."

They unloaded the ferryboat and put their wagons together. Traffic was heavy and the rains unending. They waited three days hoping the road might not be so incredibly muddy, but finally were forced to start.

Mrs. Smith now writes with a touch of desperation:

"It rains and snows. We start this morning around the portage with our wagons. We have five miles to go. I carry my babe and lead or rather carry another through the snow and mud and water almost to my knees." Apparently the four intermediate children were making the trip under their own power. "It is the worst road a team could possibly travel. I went ahead with my children and I was afraid to look behind me for fear of seeing the wagons turn over in the mud and water with everything in them. My children gave out with cold and fatigue and could not travel, and the boys had to unhitch the oxen and bring them and carry the children to camp. I was so cold and numb that I could not tell by the feeling that I had any feet at all. We started this morning at sunrise and did not get to camp until after dark and there was not one dry thread on one of us."

Their plight was truly desperate that night. To save the children they had been forced to unhitch the oxen and leave the wagon and equipment far behind. In the screaming darkness it was impossible to go after the wagon, so the entire party, babe and all, must huddle throughout the night behind a makeshift shelter. The rain drove on.

Tragedy came with the dawn. Her husband was down, too weak to rise. The unending struggle in the gorge had drained his last strength. They had reached the threshold, but too late for Smith. The boys brought up the equipment and they tried to keep him comfortable while waiting for boats to take them over the last lap.

"It is almost an impossibility to cook and quite impossible to keep warm and dry. I froze or chilled my feet so that I cannot wear a shoe, so have to go around in the cold water barefooted." Here comes her first actual complaint. Her husband was dying. Polk was dead. Welch was battling to protect his own brood. "The whole care of everything falls on my shoulders. I am not adequate to the task."

She was adequate, however, because her seven children were still alive when the boats came, nine days later. They had subsisted during the interim on beef alone. On November 27, after twenty-five days in the gorge, they arrived at Portland. The gorge had proved too long for her husband; he never arose from his bed. He died February 1, leaving Mrs. Smith alone in a strange land with her seven children.

It was not strange long. Her final record illustrates one of the phenomena of the times: the quickness with which the emigrants turned their backs on the ofttimes bitter memories of the trail, once they had reached the valley.

"I became poor as a snake," Mrs. Smith writes a little more than a year later, "but I was in good health and never so nimble since I was a child. I could run half a mile without stopping to breathe. Neither I nor my children have had a day's sickness since we came to Oregon."

This last entry includes the cheerful announcement that she is married to a Mr. Joseph Geer, himself the father of ten children, but "all married but two boys and two girls." The seventeen offspring of the combined family, seven of her own and ten of Geer's, each entitled to a square mile of the valley's free land, perhaps furnished a clue to McLoughlin's completely resigned conclusion: the rapid settlement of the country was now beyond the control of the Hudson's Bay Company.

CHAPTER VII

The Barlow Trail

Pioneers who followed the Great Migration in ever-increasing numbers were soon milling about the east entrance of the Columbia gorge like angry waters piling up behind an all too small outlet. They came by scores, hundreds, and later by thousands. By 1852 it was said that each wagon train had at least one other in sight in the close to two thousand miles of the Oregon Trail.

This human flood soon overtaxed the makeshift transportation resources of the gorge. Some parties had to wait for several weeks for passage downriver; others were forced to winter at The Dalles. It was a bonanza for speculators and sharpers. Boats could not be purchased at any price, and the haulage charges were limited only by what the traffic would bear. More and more settlers reached the valley stripped not only of their meager cash but of the near-priceless equipment they had hauled so laboriously across the continent. The river pirates held the frontier's most ruthless monopoly: it was pay or starve.

It followed naturally that the hardheaded emigrants should make a desperate effort to avoid the danger and high cost of threading the gorge. At first all such efforts failed. A wagon trail inside the gorge, following the water level, was impossible. At some points great moraines sloped down to the bank and the moving of one fragment loosened the one above, with a general landslide imminent. At other points cliffs two thousand feet high rose abruptly from deep water.

Many parties probed the barrier north and south of the gorge, but in vain. It merely cost time and blood-sweating effort; in the end the trail veered, willy-nilly, to The Dalles. One such train was snowed in at Dufur, south of the gorge, and would have perished there except that rescuers—including the sardonic river pirates—put out across the drifts from The Dalles and dragged the survivors in.

Thus the news that a wagon trail had been opened across the Cascades south of the gorge—that wagons had actually crossed it—was greeted with delight by the oncoming emigrants. It was known as the Barlow Trail, so the rumor spread across the plains. It was named after Captain Samuel K. Barlow, the "builder" of the trail. It was a toll road, operated by Barlow under a franchise from the Provisional Government, with tolls of five dollars per wagon. "Reasonable enough," voted the settlers—those who had not yet seen the road. It was much less than the charges by water. Moreover, the crossing could be made in four days, so rumor affirmed, compared to as high as a month in the terrifying gorge.

It was when the newcomers saw the "road" that new expletives rang through the timber. Nothing west of the Missouri could compare to it. The ascent to the 5000-foot crest was severe enough, particularly to oxen that had al-

ONEONTA GORGE
Mountain streams pour down through rocky gorges of the
Cascade Mountains to the sea

EAGLE CREEK "PUNCH BOWL"

Adjacent to Columbia Gorge

ready walked some two thousand miles. It was even a beautiful view westward from the top of the giant ridge. On a clear day the near edge of the valley seemed almost within rifle shot, although it was still fifty miles distant.

It was the descent on the valley side that was frightful beyond imagination. In addition to the mud, boulders, and giant trees, there was a roaring river called Zigzag which must be crossed numerous times. Zigzag sprang from the roots of the snow fields and was one long, foaming down-chute. There were numerous gorges to be threaded in the ever-dropping terrain. And finally there was famous—or infamous—Laurel Hill.

Modern tourists leave today's broad highway and tramp through the brush to stand in awe at the foot of Laurel Hill. Today's highway scales the same towering backbone of the Cascades, just south of the insular bulk of Mount Hood, and threads some of the same canyons as the Barlow Trail. But engineering genius and unlimited construction funds produced a road with no grade steeper than 12 per cent. There are spots on the mile-long Laurel Hill of the emigrants where the grade is 60 per cent.

A 60 per cent grade must be seen to be appreciated. It is considerably closer to the vertical than horizontal—roughly speaking, a cliff that leans slightly backward. Among other things, it means that while he moves forward a mile the traveler must descend more than two thousand feet. That unencumbered men and oxen could have inched down such a grade—much less any vehicle on wheels—ranks as the last and greatest feat of the emigrant trail.

Yet descend it they did, through devious and ingenious means. The signs on that scarred and terrifying slope showed that others had somehow run the gantlet. Moreover—a detail of importance to the impoverished settlers—they had already paid their admission fee, Barlow having thoughtfully placed his tollgate considerably short of the awesome jump-off.

Beyond erecting his tollgate, Barlow did little to make the incredible route passable. His name is written large on pioneer annals as the man who "built" the first wagon road across the 600-mile length of the Cascades. Actually, like Topsy, it "just grew." The pent-up waters finally found a weak point in the barrier and scoured their own channel through.

The manner in which this came about—the actual scouting of the Barlow Trail—suggests not only the implacable bulk of the range, as viewed by men who must cross it step by step, but gives a further clue to the caliber of the trail blazers themselves. There was no "federal aid" in those days, no "cradle to the grave" security. It was cross the mountains or die.

By 1845 several parties were sufficiently desperate to attempt the crossing, no matter how difficult it might prove to be. Among them was Joel Palmer, who reached The Dalles on September 30 of that year. Palmer found he must wait weeks for boat passage through the gorge. Winter was already gathering on the high desert. He persuaded several families to risk with him the crossing of the Cascades south of Mount Hood. Another group was already in the area, seeking a route. He started with fifteen wagons, overtook those ahead, and was in turn overtaken by others coming behind, until sixty wagons made up the first train, determined to force a way across the ridge. Samuel K. Barlow was a member of the party.

While this large train was hacking and inching its way toward the heights, William Rector arrived at The Dalles with his wife and seven children. He heard of the Palmer party and at once resolved to overhaul it. Rector was a forthright man, having no awe of man, beast, or mountain. His diary also reveals a wholesome disdain for the affectations of spelling, as suggested by the following excerpt:

When we arrived at the dalls, this being the end of the journey for wagons at that time, the acumulation of emgrants was allready large. The onley way posible at that time of geting from the dalls to the Willamet valey was by way of the columbia river. . . . Soon after I arived at the dalls other companys began to come in. They were in a deplorable condition, completely woren out with heardship and starvation. The suplys of provisions at the mision was well neigh exhausted.

He overtook the main party in the foothills around October 6. They were encamped, waiting apprehensively for a report from a party of scouts, including Palmer and Barlow, that had gone on ahead.

The weight of responsibility was heavy on Palmer. He was a little fearful of what lay ahead. Too many people had trusted his "hunch" and gambled with him. He and his companions ascended a creek bed for fifteen miles, scaled a steep ridge and finally came to the summit: a wide and stony plain, not yet covered with snow. Between this point and the gorge to the north the huge bulk of Mount Hood reared. Westward, far beyond and below the descending hills, they could see the glint of reflected sunlight in the well-watered valley.

It was obvious that the wagons could be brought up to this point, laborious though the ascent would be. It was decided to bring up the train, camp here, and use this as a base for scouting on the valley side. It looked simple from the crest: just a long, downgrade through the timbered gorges. . . .

Palmer was still uneasy. He scouted westward and soon came to an appalling ravine lying directly across the route. It was two or three miles wide and so deep that the timber in the depths looked tiny. The opposite slope was timbered, but the jump-off at his feet was so sheer that only a few scattered mountain laurels clung precariously to it. It angled from the base of the cloudlike peak at his right to the dim, misty distance far in the southwest.

Proceeding alone, Palmer scouted the near edge of this chasm to the great cliff at its head. His moccasins were soon worn through, but he fought on with mounting apprehension, literally barefooted in snow, rocks, and stubborn brush. It was impassable above. The icy cliff walling in the upper end of the ravine was the base of Mount Hood itself.

He returned, disregarding his bleeding feet, and descended twenty miles along the rim, seeking the lower end. But the slope became a vertical wall, and this wall joined another approaching from the east—a new river whitening the bottom of a gulf that only an eagle could have bridged. The ravine, then, must be crossed at the point from which he had first glimpsed it: where the laurels were. Unless they could be turned back, the wagons were trapped.

He hastened back to camp, having traveled close to fifty miles since breakfast, more than half that distance barefooted. He reached the wagons near midnight, and advised them to turn back at once: the route was impassable ahead. But Rector, stubborn and resolute, had just come from The Dalles. His diary records:

After informeing Palmer the condition of affairs at the dalls when I left there, I advised that we go as far as we could with the wagons . . . and that two men should go through on foot to the settlements and get fresh horses and assistance to pack through. Some of the party were not wiling to abandon their wagons. To remedy that objection I proposed that if they would open the road to the sumate pararie whare there was grass that if the wagons had to be left I would insure their safety until next June at which time the road would be opned.

This council prevailed. Having come this far, there was not much choice. Though the wagons might have to be abandoned at the summit, there was a chance that the women, children, and cattle could make it through. Better to risk this than to winter at The Dalles.

Leaving the main party to hack their way to the "sumate pararie," Rector and Barlow mounted the ridge and plunged westward to bring help from the settlements. Rector's account of this trip—the basis of Barlow's claim to having scouted the trail—brings the characters of both men into sharp focus.

We started the next morning at daylight with onley two days rations which was supposed to be ample. Barlow and Palmer had been heigh up on Mount Hood so as to overlook all the mountains and see the valey but they were not competent to judg of distance from such an elivation and thought two days was time enough to get into the valey but we found to our sorrow that it required six days to reach Oregon City. Not that the distance required six days had we known whare to go. At that time I was near forty years oald in prime of life

Barlow was my cenior by fifteen years very spry good walker but had not the botom of indurance that I had. He became very frail but did not seem to sufer with hunger as I did. I had a light shotgun but with the aproach of winter everthing had left the mountains for lower ground. So sharp was our apetites that Barlow remarked after the first days travle that he could eat all his food for super. I realy felt the same way then Barlow made a very sencible proposition that we eat just half every time and we would never get out of provisions to which I readily ascented and lived strictly up to it.

[They came to the ravine.] The second day was heard traveling a light misting rain all day. We had to descend a long wy into the kenion to get to water. It was geting dark when we got to water. In trying to start fire the matches was wet and would not make fire. We tryed the gun but that was no better. Barlow was disponding believed we would never get out of that kenion. It was very coald and raining and without fire our chances to survive was truly bad.

I got stride of a dry fallin tree with a dry lim began to rub violently, called Barlow to help. We set fase to fase on the log with a blanket over our heads and both took hold of the stick and rubed with all our power until the place was very warm then laid maches on the place to dry. In this way we succeeded in drying the maches so we got fire. I worked all night geting wood and keeping fire. Barlow slep.

After a scanty brekfast we started again but had to asend out of the kenion to the mountain side to travle. [This move put them on the eastern bank of the ravine again.] The rain had stoped but there was a heavy fog all day. After traveling several hours paralell with the kenion [going south along its edge] Barlow thought we were below the kenion and there was the valey he had seen when he was on Mount Hood. We tryed to cross but found it worse. I then determined to go no further in that direction, knowing that the cattle trail was north of us and we would chance to fall in with som one driveing catle. I had a smal compas and proposed to Barlow that we travel as near north as the country would permit until we found the catle trail to which he agreed and we started out.

Course led directly up the mountain. It was steap and tiresom. At length we got above the fog and see the mountain get heigh above us.

Here they discovered the cliff that headed the ravine, and knew that the cattle train, coming around the north side of the mountain, must be beyond this steep point. They must scale the cliff, which they did.

At length we reached the top. Here I discovered Barlow's mental faculties was failing as well as his fisical pours. He persisted in saying he had been on that identical spot before and it was not one mile from the wagon camp. [Actually it was nearer twenty-five miles.] I found that it was not posible to reach his reasoning facultys and took absolute controle of him. He complained biterly that he had to be controled, but he kept on with me.

He got frail and would frequently fall and hurt himself. I caried the axe and gun so as to relieve him of any incumberance. He walked behind me sulen and silant. Once he spoke in a kindly way and said Mr. Rector if I should brake a leg in sum of these falls what would you do with me I wuld eat you was my reply he said no more I looked around at him and see him sheding tears why Barlow you old fool I wont eat you neither will you brake a leg we will get to the trail early tomorrow but he insisted that it was very likely he would never be able to get out of these mountains and made the solem request that if he should get disabled so he could go no further that I would knock out his braines with the axe and not let him linger in pain but he took good care not to fall any more.

Well as I had predicted we got to the trail the next day and had the good luck to fall in with a partie driveing catle. We got refreshed and went on to Oregon City.

It is remarkable [Rector observes cryptically] how circumstances will change a man. When in trouble and danger he will be pias and humble but no sooner out of trouble thern his piety is gon and then ly and swair and do other nauty things.

Help came from the settlements, and the women and children were escorted to the safety of the valley. The wagons were then lowered down Laurel Hill one by one, held back by ropes anchored to the tough shrubs that clung to the face of the near precipice. Later some nameless, daring driver brought oxen and wagon down in one haul "in one piece."

The technique followed thereafter was to zigzag across the face of the slope, with all wheels locked and a tree some ten inches in diameter and forty feet long tied on behind as an additional brake. The tree was attached by the small end, so that the outspread branches gouged into the ground. At the foot of the hill the tree was abandoned, blocking the road. Complaining bitterly, the next driver would halt, unyoke his lead oxen, drag the obstruction out of the way— and leave his own tree in the same spot!

In time a great scar meandered across the face of the slope. By 1852 it was described by E. W. Conyers as follows:

The road on this hill is something terrible. It is worn down into the soil from five to seven feet deep, leaving steep banks on both sides and so narrow it is impossible to walk alongside of the cattle without leaning against the oxen.

Our wagon was all shapes coming down the hill. Sometimes one forewheel would drop nearly three feet from a boulder in the road, while at the same time the opposite rear wheel dropped two feet or more into another hole. Bad as this hill was [he concluded, philosophically], we got down in safety.

Barlow was too busy collecting tolls to spend much time on road work. The settlers were far from "choosy"; the crossing was infinitely to be preferred to the gorge route. The "take" at the tollgate was substantial by 1852. In that year, it is said, each emigrant train on the two thousand miles of the Oregon Trail was never out of sight of the column ahead or the one following behind; and most of these paid tribute to Barlow's acumen before they descended to the valley.

CHAPTER VIII

Naches Pass

Slowly the Cascades yielded to the onslaughts from the east. In 1853 the range was scaled at a second point, known as Naches Pass, north of Mount Rainier and some hundred miles north of the Columbia gorge.

This daring and near-tragic exploit was significant of the gambling caliber of the emigrants, demonstrated many times. They knew well enough, by now, that the mountains were not to be trifled with. Yet, as demonstrated in the blazing of the Barlow Trail, they were willing to risk their lives and the lives of their women and children on a new and untried route, confident that they would somehow make it through.

Community pride was partly to blame for the Naches affair. Settlers in the Puget Sound area had noted the tremendous flow of emigrants through the Columbia gorge, and the consequent rapid settlement of the Willamette Valley. Why not divert some of this flow over a northern route, and thus bring about a swifter development of the Sound country?

Citizens of Olympia accordingly banded together to hew

a road up to the timbered summit from the western side. Without waiting for the completion of this road, they dispatched a youth named Sargent to intercept a large wagon train known to be on the way and lead it northward for the attempted crossing. The theory was that the attackers from east and west would meet at the summit before snow fell.

Sargent readily agreed, notwithstanding the fact that members of his own family, his father and brothers, were in the coming train, and he had no personal knowledge of the terrain east of the pass. It had merely been "reported" that mounted Indians and a few pack trains had crossed that way.

The oncoming train as readily agreed to follow young Sargent, confident that he knew whereof he spoke. Some doubts arose when they stood in the shadow of Mount Rainier, the continent's most massive peak, and saw the remote, feathery crest north of the dome, the "low point" which must be scaled. These doubts strengthened when they ascended the wrong canyon for several miles and had to return again, losing many days. When they finally approached the summit the season was far advanced. It was too late then to turn back.

After frightful difficulties which in many ways duplicated the Barlow Trail assault, they reached the summit prairie—actually the bleak ridge above timber line—and found it empty and lifeless. No sound of axes rang in the forests that descended in stupendous steps westward; only the sustained sighing of the wind in the timber and the muted roar of hidden cataracts. It developed later that the Olympia enthusiasts had tired of their task less than a week

before. Conveniently assuming that no train was coming
this season, they had packed up and gone home.

No assumption faced the wagon train; it was brutal fact.
They had to descend before snow blanketed the Cascades.
There was no choice but to descend westward. They had
come too far to retreat to the plateau. Winter would come
first on the eastward side.

The train crept down over terrain that grew ever more
steep and treacherous, and suddenly came to a literal jump-
off. It was a vertical cliff some thirty feet high. At its bottom
was a slope so close to the perpendicular that only a few
scattered trees were rooted precariously on its thousand-
foot face. At first glance it seemed to be an impassable
barrier. Both the oxen and wagons must be lowered with
ropes down the cliff, and also down the slope. But with
what ropes?

They hit upon a desperate expedient, one that further
impaired their thin chances of survival.[1] They killed their
poorest and weakest oxen, skinned them, cut the green
hides into strips, and fashioned crude ropes deemed sufficiently strong for the purpose. The oxen and wagons were
lowered over the cliff one by one, while the anxious company watched. One wagon broke loose and went rolling
and catapulting to destruction in the gorge. But the bulk
of the train made it safely down.

In the savage terrain below, further attempts to reach
the settlements seemed vain. Still they fought on. They
came upon a pack trail, but it was too narrow for the
wagons. A road had to be hewed through the timber step

[1] An incident later dramatized in film versions of the Oregon Trail.

by step. Great logs lay across the path; they leaned smaller logs against the giants, bridged them with poles, and crept laboriously forward. They knew it was hopeless. Their food had given out. Winter was overhauling them from the heights. Sanctuary was still far below.

Then came an incident which outranks fiction. A youth from Olympia had come out with a pack train of food for the road builders. He found the camp deserted; the road builders had gone home. Leaving the food in the empty camp, he rode up the pack trail out of sheer curiosity, to "have a look at the mountains"; and thus came face to face with two emaciated white women, coming slowly down the path. Discouraged, they had walked ahead of the party, away from the wailing children and beaten men, to "have a good cry."

That slender thread bridged the gap between the party and survival. The youth brought up his food, which gave new heart and hope to the battlers of the line, then galloped back to the settlements for help. On the way he posted signs to encourage the emigrants: "This stretch is a shade better," "This stretch worse," and finally, "This is the worst."

The rest of it was a dreary, slogging, but successful race with the winter, which followed them down like whitened wolves from the heights. The road makers came up from Olympia and helped the train through. The wagons crossed the Greenwater River sixteen times during the descent, the White six times. Following a final haul over a swirling ridge known as Wind Mountain, they came at last to the sea-level flats and sanctuary. There might be rain and fog here during the "winter months," even an occasional blanket of transient snow. But the drifts and blizzards and subzero winds sweeping the Great Plains—all that "winter" truly meant to unprotected wagons east of the Cascades—now lay beyond the sheltering barrier.

CHAPTER IX

Pirates of the Gorge

FOLLOWING the Naches Pass saga, other wagon trails precariously threaded the once "unscalable" mountains, notably at the Mackenzie and Santiam passes, which were old Indian trails far to the south. But the wagon trains attacking these points comprised only a trickle compared to those passing the Barlow tollgate, and Barlow's peak business, in turn, was dwarfed by the ever-mounting traffic rolling through the Columbia gorge. The law of gravity being inexorable, the greatest volume of men and goods flowed through the only break in the barrier as naturally as the river itself.

It proved to be a golden tide for transportation "pirates" who quickly flocked to the scene. A modern school of thought holds that the monopolistic instinct is peculiar to "economic royalists" and "malefactors of great wealth." The history of the Columbia gorge traffic shows it to be a garden variety of human selfishness. The very men who suffered the hardships of the plains were the first to set up shop at the giant threshold to the free land and levy tribute on those who followed.

The gorge was almost ideally suited to the business of making travelers pay through the nose. The peak traffic invariably came in the fall, when high rates meant little compared to passing the gateway before snow flew. Once in the cleft, the traveler had no choice but to utilize the transportation offered. River boats had to be used in the middle stretch, between The Dalles and the cascades at the western threshold, since the walls on either side were sheer. At the cascades, in turn, the portage road could not be avoided. All in all, it was a perfect setup for the shoals of cutthroats who soon swarmed along the fifty-mile corridor.

This was discovered long before the white man came, by a hard-bitten and shifty tribe of Indians called Wahclellahs, who nested like watchful buzzards at the foot of the great cliffs, and in a slovenly village at the water's edge above the cascades. The Wahclellahs lived off the country, but the butter on their bread, so to speak, came from levying tribute on travelers going through the gap. It was robbery disguised as "assistance" through the gorge. They were skilled boatmen and packers and they alone knew the vagaries of the current and the easiest portage trails.

They had maintained themselves comfortably for generations by preying on the thin Indian travel through the gorge, but when the white man came, beginning with the Lewis and Clark Expedition in 1805 and on to the swelling emigrant tide in the middle of the century, the Wahclellahs really came into an inheritance. Early voyageurs and trappers were easy prey. The Wahclellahs demanded, and received, extravagant wages for piloting through the swift water and for packing goods and boats around the cascades portage. Much of the equipment was conveniently "lost"

in transit. The more closefisted emigrants found them waiting there, arrogant and thievish, and must choose between
hiring them, fighting them, or paying to be left in peace.

As soon as the traffic warranted it, however, these primitive racketeers were replaced by a hardier breed—the white
men themselves. The dispossessed Wahclellahs looked on
in envy and awe from the banks during the next two decades
following the middle fifties; they learned, too late, some of
the finer points in a game as old as human traffic.

The first era saw a combination of steamboat and portage
interests warring among themselves but reaching complete
agreement on one key point, which was to charge all the
traffic would bear. It soon became a two-way traffic, as gold
mining and stock raising opened up east of the mountains,
and vast wheat regions began to be plowed on the high, dry
inland plateau. The gorge could not have been designed
more neatly for the purposes of the "pirates."

The traveler upriver from Portland, for example, rode
by steamboat to the foot of the cascades. There he trans-
ferred to a stagecoach for the nine-mile portage past the
white water, and again boarded a river boat plying through
the middle stretch to The Dalles. At Celilo Falls—the
twenty-foot shelf mentioned by the Applegate diary—the
traveler again rode on shore for a few miles, while behind
him crawled the freight wagons carrying the cargo. This
time, when he boarded the waiting river boat, travel was un-
obstructed for hundreds of miles into the "inland empire."

Naturally the portages and docks within the gorge were
immensely valuable. Since there was nothing to prevent new
fleets of steamboats from plying the stream itself, the
portages were the true monopoly. Whoever managed to

obtain title to them became—temporarily, at least, as long as he could defend his title—a rich man. Short railroads soon replaced the slower wagon trains over these land hauls, the rights of way still being in private hands.

Rival owners on each side of the river kept their charges within limits of a sort, though the tariff through the gorge was the major portion of freight costs on the entire river run. They had traffic by the throat but could not agree on the division of the spoils. A flood which drowned out the north portage was like manna from heaven to the south-bank owners; the two speculators who had purchased the south-bank portage charged passengers exorbitant prices to pass, whether they were carried on the cars or walked the entire distance.

Finally, in self-defense, the steamship companies merged and bought out the rights of way on both banks, and the monopoly was complete. New reduced rates were announced with a considerable fanfare, and traffic boomed. But the temptation was too great. Gradually the charges rose until the cost of the fifty miles through the gorge was greater than for the remaining four hundred miles upriver.

Great fortunes were made during the golden decades which ended in 1880. They were golden for the operators, a nightmare for the public. The men who pooled their resources and formed the steamship companies were simple, hard-working pioneers. Short seasons later the same men were "economic royalists." A river boat could pay for itself five times over in a single season.

Bizarre devices were used to treble and even quadruple the published rates, particularly at the expense of the emigrants. The method of computing the freight to be assessed against a wagon, for instance, is illuminating. Its width was measured, then its length, with tongue extended. Then the tongue was raised to the vertical to measure the height. These maximum distances were then multiplied together, the result being the "cubic space" occupied by the wagon. After the dazed emigrant had paid the charge the tongue was removed, slung under the wagon, and other freight piled on top.

The railroads came about 1880, breathing ruin and destruction for the "pirates of the gorge," and blasted out roadbeds along the base of the massive cliffs. The steamship company was, in fact, ruined. Profits fell to the point where steamship travel virtually ceased. Traffic boomed again. Another new "era of prosperity" had been ushered in.

But a goose which lays golden eggs, it appears, always has a long and inviting neck. The insidious urge to wring that neck soon overpowered the railroads. Achieving a meeting of minds on rates without difficulty, they raised those rates slowly until the "take" outstripped anything the pirates had dared to squeeze from the long-suffering traffic. The federal Government—the final authority on "the public interest"—stepped in (this was in 1896) and built locks which enabled river traffic to by-pass the cascades and run up through the gorge to The Dalles, where freight wagons could fan out into the interior country independent of rail transportation.

Later—in 1915—another federal bureau built a canal around Celilo Falls, at the eastern end of the gorge, and the river thus was entirely open throughout its navigable length. Still later, highways through the gorge opened the way for motorbus, truck, and private car, a new traffic route independent of both river and railroad. When airliners began to wing through the cleft, oblivious to all obstacles that harass earthbound trails, the era of monopolies in the gorge was deemed to have closed.

And yet, just prior to the beginning of World War II there came a curious development in the gorge. In it may be the seeds of the final "squeeze." Many a forthright descendant of pioneers insists that the monopolistic hand of steel is plain enough in its silken glove of "public interest." Others, as vociferously, assert that a great monument to an enlightened age has been built, to the eternal benefit of posterity.

This refers to the Bonneville Dam, which spans the gorge just below the cascades. The immense structure was completed in 1937, its final generator installed late in 1943. One federal agency financed it, a second built it, a third operates it. It was begun as a Federal Works project during the depression. Its total cost was in excess of $81,000,000, plus an item of $72,000,000 for a power transmission system, later appended, or a total above $150,000,000. This cost has been charged to flood control, river navigation, and other "public benefits," including hydroelectric power.

Thus far the major public benefit has come from the power, some 500,000 kilowatts of it. A navigation lock with the world's highest lift was included at a cost in excess of $5,000,000, on the theory that deep-sea navigation would thus extend as far as The Dalles. At this writing, for show purposes, one freighter has been escorted to The Dalles. Flood benefits have been nil, since the dam is little more than an obstruction in the current, and the full flow of the river passes either through the generators or over the spillway.

Thus the burden of justifying the existence of the huge structure falls upon its power output alone. The Bonneville Power Administration—the federal bureau in charge—has fixed a low consumer rate on the 500,000-kilowatt output, asserts that this is "cheap power" produced by public funds, and the public is therefore entitled to its benefits. To make sure that the public receives this cheap power, the Administration insists, it may be necessary—and probably will be "in the public interest"—to either buy out the private power companies in the area or build duplicating transmission systems. In any event, the private companies must go.

Defenders of the private companies, on the other hand, insist vehemently that the term "cheap power" is a complete misnomer, since the rate fixed by the Administration bears no remote relation to the cost of the power. They point out that the actual cost of the dam has been disregarded in fixing the rates, and that the expense of administration—at this writing a far greater percentage of gross revenue than that of any known private company—is likewise disregarded. Furthermore, these defenders of free enterprise insist, the consumer rates in effect prior to the building of Bonneville Dam were already less than one half the rates paid throughout the balance of the nation. Since the consumer would actually pay more for Bonneville "cheap power"—out of the steadily enlarging pocket labeled "federal taxes"—in what theoretical and perhaps sinister philosophy is this "public interest" rooted?

Whatever the merits of the controversy, the dam is there, colossal and permanent. From the water's edge it is at least a mighty monument to man's engineering genius, a symbol of a modern era far removed from that marked by the dust banner of the emigrants along the trackless horizon. From the cliffs the dam seems frailer, the river larger. From the peaks it is a mere line drawn across a current which the Cascades themselves had also attempted, vainly, to halt.

All man-made changes in the gorge have been slight compared to the size of the cleft and the changeless bulk of the mountains. The threshold is easier to pass today, with ribbons of steel threading each side of the gorge; with twin highways blasted from the opposite cliffs; with river boats on the current and passenger planes shuttling above. The great barrier would seem to have been completely humbled at last.

And still the pagan gods must have returned briefly to their empty thrones, less than two decades ago, and enjoyed a quiet chuckle. A storm from the east and a warm wind from the west met above the range, head on, causing the heaviest snowfall in years along the length of the Cascades. A thaw followed, causing snowslides which obliterated the highways and railroads in the gorge. Then came a severe freeze, solidifying the mass.

The net result was that all rail and highway traffic ceased. Ice floes from the interior jammed the gorge, so that river traffic was impossible. All telegraph and telephone lines were down, all airplanes grounded. For twenty-six days the eastward plateau was as isolated from the Pacific slope as it had been a century before—a sign, perhaps, that man's "mighty" works are like the gossamer threads that glitter so bravely—and so fleetingly—in the niches and crannies of the gorge's eternal cliffs.

CHAPTER X

Highways

WITH THE COMING of the railroads in the eighties, a new wave of settlers poured into the Pacific Northwest and spread out on both sides of the Cascades as the ambitions and tastes of the individual dictated. It was solely a matter of choice in those gala days. The areas were huge; there was plenty of room. New prospects beckoned at the end of each existing road.

Great cattle and wheat ranches soon blanketed the eastern plateau, permeated by irrigation projects along the high, fertile valleys. Into the Pacific slope hurried the dairyman, the orchardist, the lumberman, the manufacturer. Industries mushroomed. New settlements dotted the valleys. Portland was soon the world's largest lumber manufacturing center, an honor for which Tacoma, on Puget Sound, was presently battling. Seattle became the roaring gateway to Alaska and the Orient. It was the era of expansion, of consolidation of pioneer gains.

Above all this bustle and chaos—the growing pains of empire—the Cascades towered more massively and inscrutably than before. Because human currents also follow the path of least resistance, and first flood the lower levels, the range became, in effect, an almost unbroken island six hundred miles long, and from fifty to a hundred miles wide, marooned in restless seas. Valleys were settled only up to the point where the timbered slopes began, and except for the pioneer routes, over which wagon travel quickly dwindled, roads from east and west turned back at the cliffs. The most accessible peaks were soon scaled, since their challenge could not be denied. When the lumbering and logging era began—a saga in itself—surveyors threaded the outer fringes of the nation's mightiest stand of virgin timber. A few miners, geologists, and hunters mounted occasionally and laboriously to the timber line.

But up to the turn of the century, except for these scattered attacks, the great barrier still divided east from west as completely as in pioneer days. The continent's last range to be discovered also yielded most slowly to exploration. It was only by degrees, and resulting from many diverse urges rooted in both pleasure and profit, that the tremendous wealth of the Cascades—material, scenic, and recreational—gradually became known.

The inventory is not yet complete. One of the unique features of the Cascades is that, while its timber and hydroelectric resources have been appraised, its geology analyzed in general, and its major peaks scaled, the unexplored still outranks the explored by far. There are nests of well-surveyed terrain about each peak, through portions of the great national parks, and along stretches of the major east-west highways of today. In between lie thousands of square miles of untouched wilderness.

Modern maps, for example, show the whole area of the

Cascades laid out in neat squares, but many of these lines have never been surveyed. It was done by triangulation, from bench mark to bench mark across sometimes impassable canyons. Today's modern highways scale the ridge at eleven separate points, including two in the gorge. At scores of places on each of these highways untouched wilds are within rifle shot. An aviator who crashed in the Cascades in the early twenties required five days to reach civilization. In that five days he did not see a single trail or mark to indicate that man had ever passed that way. Aerial surveys of less than a decade ago revealed numerous lakes whose prior existence was unknown.

Two things broke down the age-old aloofness of the Cascades. The coming of the automobile brought the range nearer to growing centers of population. This caused a demand for highways which would not only penetrate but scale the barrier. The clamor was loudest from the inland plateau, still barred from the Pacific slope by the absence of anything remotely resembling an automobile road.

But highways meant more taxes, and the tax load made necessary by all the myriad demands of a growing community was already heavy. Moreover, distances were vast in the Northwest. Who was to pay the bill?

The device hit upon has been cursed heartily by more than one motorist, and was fought in the beginning by the oil companies and automobile manufacturers and other viewers with alarm. It was the gasoline tax, which originated in Oregon, was quickly copied by the state of Washington, and later spread to every state in the union. By the simple expedient of placing the burden on the one who enjoyed its benefits, the motorist, a whole new era of road building was ushered in.

The famed Columbia River Highway, on the south bank of the gorge, was the first major route for automobile travel blasted through or across the Cascades. It began at Portland, below the west threshold of the Columbia gorge, and the outstandingly scenic portion of it ends at The Dalles, the eastern entrance to the great cleft. It presented tremendously difficult problems, from the very nature of the gorge. Sheer cliffs two thousand feet high arose at some points directly from the water. At others the walls were broken, and vast moraines sloped up sharply to the mile-high timbered slopes. One precipice might be solid basalt, the next crumbling and insecure. Narrow canyons thrust in at right angles to the river. They were too wide to be bridged at the crest, yet the sole route at the river's edge had already been taken over by the railroads.

Veteran road builders shook their heads after a preliminary survey and said flatly that it couldn't be done. Nevertheless, the funds were appropriated and a noted engineer, Samuel C. Lancaster, decided to make the project the crowning effort of his career. Because of the myriad problems involved, a commission headed by Lancaster toured both hemispheres, studying the world's major mountain routes.

An amusing incident occurred on this tour, later retold in scores of modified forms. One of the civilian members of Lancaster's commission was a prominent Portland merchant whose education included many of the intricacies of retail trade but was somewhat lacking in such details as history and architecture. He was of the enthusiastic executive type, ready and eager to make quick, sweeping decisions.

Such a decision confronted him in Italy. An Italian

engineer was escorting the party. In the hills above Naples they came upon an excellent example of dry masonry, designed to protect the highway against erosion from the adjacent slope.

"Stop!" shouted the Portland enthusiast. The limousine obediently stopped. "There—that's the stuff we want, exactly! Who built it? We'll hire him to duplicate it out there in the gorge. Has he got a reputation?"

"He is quite well known," admitted the Italian engineer. "But——"

"It doesn't matter. He's hired. Who is he?"

"That is the difficulty," said the Italian. "The builder, he is no longer here. His name was Julius Caesar."

In spite of the unavailability of history's master road builder, duplicates of the Caesarian dry masonry today border the gorge highway at points subjected to slides, and have successfully functioned during their first quarter of a century.

After preliminary studies were concluded, no expense was spared in the actual construction. The result ranks among the highway masterpieces of the world. It has been said that no verbal description can do justice to the Columbia River Highway. It is one of those rarest of human achievements, where engineering technique has decorated rather than defaced a natural and massively beautiful setting.

In brief, Lancaster's corps of specialists appraised each contour and vertical dimension with an eye to both utility and beauty. When it was necessary to blast across the face of a cliff the ledge was buttressed with massive stone-masonry hewed from the wall itself. At times, as at Crown

Point, at the western threshold of the gorge, the highway is seven hundred feet above the river. Again, paralleling the cascades, it is at the water's edge, at the base of waterfalls plunging down from the heights. One of these, Multnomah Falls, drops a sheer seven hundred and twenty-four feet.

There are many of these frail and beautiful cataracts, some suspended in dells and timbered ravines glimpsed only fleetingly, so that no motorist sees them all in a single trip. The vast majority of travelers through the gorge have missed Bridal Veil, since the crest is at the highway's edge and its foam-flecked receiving basin almost out of sight below. Only the few have pulled up at the roadside and entered Oneonta Gorge—a cleft so narrow that it can almost be spanned by the outstretched arms—and so into a cathedrallike amphitheater all too tritely and ineptly named the Devil's Punch Bowl.

During the numerous ascents and descents from crest to water's edge the convolutions of the highway are hidden in the timber. One of these, called the Loops, which lifts the westbound motorist gradually up to magnificent Crown Point, was among scores of details labeled "impossible" on paper. It is an engineering jewel appreciated only by the expert. From the opposite bank it appears incredible. First a car is seen bowling along at the river's edge. Seconds later it is creeping blandly around Crown Point, tiny against the sky.

Almost without exception, motorists stop at Crown Point to survey the finest view obtainable along the Columbia's 1200-mile length. It is also the first full glimpse of the Pacific slope. From this point on, its once uneasy waters resting at last, the great river slides the final placid one hun-

dred and twenty-five miles to the sea. The view westward is
tranquil: an ever-green, rolling terrain which extends to the
distant coast hills and flattens out gradually into the immense
Willamette Valley, still far to the southwest. Always striking to the modern traveler—though not so poignantly as to
the trail-scarred emigrants of a century ago—is the air of
drowsy, benevolent well-being abroad over hill and valley.
It is obvious from the lush vegetation alone, which extremes
of heat or cold would have withered long since, that here
begins the land where "storms never blow."

North and south from Crown Point the mountains still
block out the sky. Eastward is a forty-mile segment of the
once formidable gorge—formidable still when winter rolls
in blindingly from the east, to dwindle and die in swirling
air currents here at the threshold. The force of those currents at the 700-foot level is rarely felt in the valley below.
In the touring-car era more automobile tops were blown off
at Crown Point than anywhere eastward on the transcontinental route.

It was below this lofty spot, almost a century ago, that
Mrs. Elizabeth Smith wrote in her diary, while her husband
lay dying and her chilled brood huddled about her: "The
whole care of everything falls upon my shoulders. I am not
adequate to the task." She had underestimated her resources;
her children's children built Crown Point.

Following the building of another highway on the north
bank of the gorge, less scenic but even more useful as a
traffic artery than its predecessor, other great motor highways soon penetrated sections of the range previously
viewed only by timber cruisers, hunters, and that greatest

and most diligent of all explorers, the itinerant prospector.

The Snoqualmie Pass and Chinook Pass routes, north of Rainier, scale the barrier through a series of rough, heavily timbered gorges, the former dipping down into Seattle's suburbs via beautiful Snoqualmie Falls. Portions of the Chinook Pass route follow the same canyon mounted so wearily by the wagon train previously described.

South of the gorge the Wapinita Cutoff comes in at an angle from the eastern plateau and scales the crest at the very base of Mount Hood, at the "sumate pararie" mentioned in Rector's diary. The descent on the westward side gives the traveler a glimpse of the appalling grades down which countless wagons were lowered during the heyday of the Barlow Trail.

Still farther south is a highway unique in both utility and beauty: the Mackenzie Pass. Prior to its opening, in the twenties, motorists from the high central Oregon region who wished to visit the Willamette Valley, some eighty air miles distant across the range, must travel north to the gorge and return on the west side, a round trip of more than three hundred and fifty miles. The route today lies due west, scaling the ridge at the base of three beautiful peaks known as "The Sisters," and threading the most desolate stretch of the Cascades: the Mackenzie lava fields.[1]

Five more highways scale the southern section of the long barrier: the North and South Santiam, Willamette, Crater Lake, and Klamath Falls highways. The first three are beautiful routes, though less spectacular than those on the north. The Crater Lake Highway provides access to one of the scenic gems of the range. The Klamath route more

[1]See Chapter XVI, "Geology of the Cascades."

literally circles the southern end of the range, threading the promontories and cliffs which descend by degrees into the lesser chaos of the Siskiyous.

The opening of these east-west highways, plus federally built roads serving the national parks and forest reserves, not only gave new access to material wealth but brought closer many new summer and winter playgrounds throughout the length of the range. In particular it brought the common man nearer to the crowning glory of the Cascades, its giant peaks.

CHAPTER XI

Mount Rainier

UNIQUE among all mountain ranges is the manner in which each of the Cascades' lofty peaks stands alone: a glittering and stately procession which extends from Mount Baker, near the Canadian border, to the little-known McLoughlin, just north of the California line. Ten individual peaks rear above the 10,000-foot level in that 500-mile column of giants. It is only for a short time in midwinter that the entire length of the ridge is whitened; during most of the year each of the great monoliths stands marooned and aloof in its ever-green setting.

Mount Rainier, the highest peak in the Cascades—higher than any peak in the Rocky Mountains and the third highest in North America—reaches an altitude of 14,408 feet above sea level. It is the continent's most massive individual mountain, one of the most enormous single masses of rock reared above the globe's surface. Visible from most points in Washington and from many points in Oregon, more than one hundred miles distant, and from far out to sea, it was a natural challenge to adventurous white men from the be-

MOUNT RAINIER

The continent's most massive peak, from "Indian Henry's
Hunting Ground"

MOUNT RAINIER

Mount Rainier, on sky line, monarch of the northwest, rears its great snow dome 14,000 feet into the sky. Viewed from the spectacular ice cliffs near the summit of Mount St. Helen's, thirty miles away

ginning. Many early attempts to reach its crest failed. The Indians themselves would have no part of it.

In 1870 an outdoor enthusiast appropriately named "Hazard" Stevens and his pal, P. B. Van Trump, determined to tame Rainier. They persuaded Sluiskin, a local Indian celebrity, to guide them. But Sluiskin had notions of his own: the white men should be protected from their own folly. He led them over a roundabout, terrific route which ended on a lookout point high on a bleak ridge. From there the full majesty of the peak was before them, filling the sky. Eloquently Sluiskin pleaded with them not to approach closer to the awful High Place where the spirits dwelt. Should they do so, he asserted, avalanches and great winds would sweep them away. It was death to go farther.

Unconvinced, the two white men tried to persuade Sluiskin to carry on. But the Indian chanted a dirge for them, took solemn leave, and abandoned them to their fate.

The resolute pair continued their assault. It required eleven hours to find a route up the final slope. Avalanches thundered by them and the great winds blew, as Sluiskin had warned. Night overtook them, short of the summit, but they found a series of steam vents issuing from the bleak north side. The heat had melted a cavern in the eternal ice. They crept inside for forty feet, built a wall of stones about a steam jet, and spent the night protected from the freezing wind, but none too comfortable in the damp, sulphur-impregnated cave.

The next day, the spirits being kind or asleep, they reached the crest and looked out upon ten thousand square miles of as beautiful and variegated scenery as the continent affords. The same day they made it safely back to timber line.

Many climbers have since made the ascent. It is the sheer bulk of the mountain, rather than any unusual hazards, which crosses it from the amateur's casual list of "things to do this week end." No vertical cliffs nor abysses to be crossed with ropes bar the way. Under favorable weather conditions it is possible to ascend and descend the same day, but the usual custom is to go up in the evening to Camp Muir—elevation 10,000 feet—spend the night, and begin early the following morning to skirt a sheer wall from which the morning sun sends down showers of icicles and rocks. Once this danger point is passed the climber threads his way among the crevasses and snow mounds for almost two miles before the summit is reached. Most amateurs are satisfied with achieving Camp Muir, though the view from the summit is incomparably more magnificent.

The mountain is enclosed in a national park area, one of twenty-two national parks in continental United States, Alaska, and Hawaii. It is dedicated to the public in perpetuity, which means that as long as the American way of living persists the area surrounding the peak will be kept as nearly as possible in the state in which it was first viewed by Stevens and Van Trump. This area is eighteen miles square, and from it the white dome of Rainier rises 10,000 feet, crested and clothed with eternal snow. The dome is wide-based and rounded, so that to sailors viewing it from a hundred miles out to sea—their first glimpse of the continent—it thrusts up slowly from the horizon line like a roughhewn, silvery fragment of the moon itself. Glaciers work their way slowly down those colossal slopes, kept alive by scores of feet of new snow each season. Each melts at timber line into a rushing river that appears full-grown from beneath the ice or seeps into lower mountain lakes which feed yet other rivers.

There is near-by beauty in those awesome dimensions. Alpine meadows, vivid with hundreds of varieties of flowers which bloom during July and August, encircle the peak and comprise a vast, upsloping garden in the area known as Paradise Park. Wind-twisted and snow-dwarfed alpine trees dot the meadows. The entire park is a sanctuary for birds and animals, with hunting prohibited, logging forbidden, and deer, elk, mountain sheep, and black bear roaming the summer slopes without fear.

The tourist today easily ascends by motor to a point higher than the one which the Indian guide, Sluiskin, dared not pass. Two highways approach Rainier from opposite sides. An east-west route crosses via Chinook Pass, just north of the peak, at an altitude of 5440 feet, then dips down to join US-99, the Canada-to-Mexico highway known as the world's "longest unbroken pavement." This is for the casual visitor, intent only on a good view of the mountain.

For those who wish a close acquaintance with the giant peak, the area known as Paradise Park, on the southwest side, is the true threshold. It is approached directly from Tacoma, or over a network of market roads that feed into the park highway. The drive from Tacoma takes less than two hours and is the only approach to Rainier that is kept open throughout the winter. Year-round accommodations for outdoor enthusiasts are available, both at Longmire's, a hot springs resort, and at Paradise Inn, at the edge of beautiful Paradise Valley.

Winter sports reach their pinnacle on the giant slopes above Paradise Valley. The snow lies twenty feet deep in midseason, offering what experts assert is the finest ski terrain in the nation. Ski schools are maintained, and each week end has its calendar of races and other contests. In midsummer the enthusiasts merely climb a little higher to reach the eternal snow fields.

For those who wish merely to contemplate the mountain, the scene outspread from the steps of the inn is one of perpetual and ever-changing grandeur. Alpine meadows are in the foreground, riotous with color. In the higher mass of the peak rainbow-hued ice caves and crevasses break the face of the glacier. Still higher, yet seemingly close in the crystalline air, loose particles of snow and ice appear to trickle slowly over a ledge. It is only when the air shakes to deep-toned thunders that the true meaning of it comes home. It is a substantial avalanche, tumbling down a thousand-foot cliff; a mighty force of nature made puny only by distance and the background of the enormous peak.

A vigorous controversy about Rainier's height raged when Californians began to assert that the Sierra's Mount Whitney should have the honor of being known as the loftiest in continental United States. The crown was juggled back and forth, depending on the survey. The "final" computation, weighty and painstaking, found Whitney's crest topping Rainier by eighty-eight feet. Cascade enthusiasts had the last word, however; they pointed out that Rainier's bulk could absorb at least eight Whitneys. Moreover, they assert, Rainier is no mere "highest crag" among a series, but stands solitary and dominant, with some eight thousand feet of its vast dome rising majestically above the surrounding terrain.

The debate over Rainier's height was a polite exchange

compared to the brawl later set off by the suggestion that the ancient Indian name of "Tacoma" be used instead of the name "Rainier," bestowed by Captain Vancouver in 1792. The hustling city of Tacoma proposed it; Seattle led the outcry against it. The resultant civil war turned friend against friend, divided families, and almost precipitated riots. Echoes of the battle resounded ponderously in the state legislature and in the halls of Congress. When the decade's most colossal tempest in a teapot had subsided, the mountain was still there, vast and undisturbed. Its official name is still Rainier, though flames of battle smolder on, and more than one embittered Tacoma veteran is keeping his powder dry.

CHAPTER XII

Mount Hood

Hordes of admirers are ready to leap to the defense of each of the Cascades' major peaks: the ten whose crests pierce the clouds drifting at the 10,000-foot level. To compare one with the other is to invite disaster. Nevertheless superlatives can be applied to two without serious dissension: Mount Rainier and Mount Hood. The former is unquestionably America's most massive peak; the latter—in the opinion of a majority of world-traveled observers—the most beautiful.

By far the most common expression from those who first see Mount Hood, viewed from any angle, is: *"That's what a mountain should look like!"* More than one artist has looked at the peak wonderingly, for the first time, with the puzzled feeling that he had seen it before. The truth is that he had actually painted it before, brushing in these same delicate yet stately proportions—the contour, the mass, the near-perfect composition and color combinations—certain, deep in his heart, that no such mountain existed.

To the emigrants creeping westward along the Oregon Trail it was not only a startlingly beautiful peak which towered higher above the plateau with each day's march, but the signpost marking the last mountains and the ominous Columbia gorge. Once it was behind them, their trail work was done. Thereafter, from the valley side, it was a constant, benevolent reminder that the heartbreak of the plains was now far away.

It rises up directly from the range just south of the Columbia gorge. The backbone of the Cascades here is some 4000 feet above sea level, and above this ever-green foundation the snowy, clean-cut pyramid soars up another mile and a half to a total height of 11,245[1] feet. Because of its superb proportions the peak seems frail, almost fragile, yet its base is actually close to seven miles in diameter. Vivid color contrasts enhance its unique beauty: the green of the timber, the white of the snow fields, the blue of the sky. A trick of lofty air currents adds the final touch. Almost daily throughout the long summer, though the sky may be completely flawless elsewhere, a single cloud trails like a white streamer from the topmost crag.

It is often thought that this phenomenon is responsible for the mountain's name. Actually it was named in 1792 by Lieutenant Broughton, of Vancouver's command, in honor of Rear Admiral Hood of His Majesty's Navy. Sporadic "movements" arise from time to time to change this British name to one of local origin, but the effort always proves too great. Too many other points were labeled by the industrious Vancouver and his helpers, including Puget Sound, Hood's Canal, Vashon Island, Port Orchard, Port Townsend, Whitby Island, Bellingham Bay, and the Cascades peaks Baker, Rainier, and St. Helens in addition to Hood.

[1]All mountain elevations from United States Coast and Geodetic Survey.

Moreover, paraphrasing Shakespeare's inquiry about the rose, Hood's admirers ask: "Would it be more beautiful under any other name?"

It is not a remote and austere beauty. On the contrary, Hood is the most easily accessible of the continent's great peaks, and by far the easiest to climb. This, in turn, makes it one of the most popular of the Cascades' winter and summer playgrounds. During normal times as many as two thousand men, women, and children scale the peak each summer, and many thousands more permeate all corners of the forest reserve that guards its base.

Near at hand the mountain is far from frail. Its immense snowy slopes offer safe climbing routes for the amateur on the south side, while the assault from the north and east tests the skill of the most daring mountaineer. Similarly the winter sports attract novice and expert alike, with ski fields safe for the beginner and more difficult runs fit for championship meets, all served by ski lifts, shelter cabins, inns, and highways skirting the timber line.

It is less than a two-hour drive from Portland to the edge of the snow fields. The highway (the Wapinita Cutoff, previously mentioned) leaves the valley floor and mounts up through rolling foothills past the Bull Run watershed, source of Portland's famed water supply. This water, composed of melted snow, is so chemically pure that it is fed to infants and is used in storage batteries and for numerous laboratory purposes without distillation. There are many streams of similar water dashing down through the forest. The highway crosses many of them, including Zigzag, the bane of the covered wagons, whose stream is still milk-white from the leaching snow, and enters the Mount Hood National Forest.

The forest reserve is maintained in its natural state, except for trails and camp facilities. Summer cottages line the highway and side roads, built on leased federal land. It is an area whose natural beauty is enhanced by a profusion of wild rhododendron and vine maple. The road soon mounts up the final ramparts, passing close by the tollgate erected by Barlow a century ago, and so comes out on the backbone of the range. It is still below timber line, but to the north the huge bulk of the mountain fills the sky.

This high point is called Government Camp, a settlement lined with public inns, ski lodges, and other places of business catering to year-round vacationists, as well as to highway travel. The highway itself is still a thousand feet below the snow fields, which hang like clouds above the timber. Up yonder is Timberline Lodge, a magnificent hostelry thronged with sports enthusiasts during the season. The lodge is connected with the highway by an excellent motor road, and from it a ski lift takes the vacationist the final thousand-foot jump skyward to the perpetual snow.

Leaving Government Camp, the highway dips down into the southeast to reach the inland plateau, but a secondary route branches to the left, or north, rejoins the Columbia River Highway, and thus completely encircles the base of the mountain. This is called the Mount Hood Loop Highway. The complete circuit over the Loop from Portland—up the Columbia gorge to Hood River, thence south around the base of the mountain via famed Hood River Valley to Government Camp and return to Portland—can be done easily by motor in six hours, and is ranked among the finest scenic mountain routes in America.

Even the magnificence of the gorge is outdone by the constantly changing views of Mount Hood during the giant swing over the Loop. Since the motorist is proceeding clockwise in a rough circle, the peak at the center of the circle is constantly at his right. It is not continuously in view. Headlands and timbered bluffs occasionally intervene, then the mountain reappears again in a new lighting effect as the slanting sunlight is thrown back in dazzling brilliance from the slowly wheeling glacier and ice cliff.

Between these overpowering glimpses of the peak an ever-changing panorama unfolds both near and far. At times a ravine drops away more than one thousand feet from the highway's edge. Distant streams and lakes twinkle briefly in the timber. The white peaks to the north, Adams and St. Helens, hang high above a sea of green. Again, at a bend in the road, the stately profile of the Cascades southward is in view, with Mount Jefferson seemingly near at hand, though forty miles distant—and the tiny triple spires of the Three Sisters leaning down over the very edge of the horizon, more than a hundred miles away.

Among the scores of scenic gems adjacent to the Loop is flawless Lost Lake. The cold blue waters of this forest pool, fed by melting snow from the higher slopes and generally protected from air currents by the surrounding terrain, comprise a natural mirror in which Mount Hood's reflection has been photographed countless times. Famous color photographers have asserted that plates made at Lost Lake, showing both the peak and its perfect reflection in the water, constitute the ultimate in that much-debated attribute known as "composition." Yet the greatest of these artists always emerges from his darkroom, muttering. The most advanced and exacting techniques of photography fail to catch all the color harmonies of lake, forest, mountain, and sky to which the photographer himself thrilled when he pressed the shutter.

Lost Lake was a favorite Indian summer camp for centuries before the white man "discovered" it. The red man may have been aware of the beauty of the surroundings, though lacking the means to impart it. The prime attractions were the lush huckleberries and mountain blackberries which blanketed the mountain slopes. Legend says that while a tribe were encamped there, enjoying a feast of berries and fresh venison, a milk-white doe burst through the group, with wolves in hot pursuit, plunged into the lake, and disappeared beneath the blue waters. This caused the lake to be pronounced "bad medicine" by tribal authorities, a taboo that was heeded for many seasons.

Finally members of the tribe, gaining courage from the white man's disdain of taboos, began to steal back surreptitiously to the lake. The Cascades boasted of no finer huckleberries than those on adjacent banks. Then, in 1912, occurred an incident which revived the ancient fears. A young Indian couple, educated in the white man's schools, decided to flout the taboo openly and spend their honeymoon in this most beautiful spot. A storm came up one day, they stood beneath a tree for shelter, and the bride was killed by a bolt of lightning. The Indians now shun the lake, though white men throng there in increasing numbers each season.

The ascent of Mount Hood, in midwinter, is one of the most perilous on the globe. Many lives have been lost in the attempt, and scarcely a season passes without another name or group of names being added to the long list of those who yearned to be the first in the new year to reach the summit, and failed. Authorities frown upon it, yet new recruits constantly thirst for the ephemeral honor.

The danger lies in the sudden savage storms which break like surf along the length of the Cascades when the winter chill of the inland plateau collides with the warmth of the Pacific slope. No experienced mountaineer ever attempts the winter climb if the crest of the peak is hidden. From below, the clouds may seem to be wheeling lazily up yonder, but the force and fury of the blasts scouring the crags is indescribable. To attempt the climb on a cloudless winter day is a formidable gamble, though the crest can be reached in eight hours and the actual distance traversed is only 3.7 miles from timber line. That time interval is enough for a winter storm to blow in from the east. Once caught in the teeth of it, few have emerged.

During the summer season, by contrast, Mount Hood becomes the easiest and least dangerous to scale of any of the continent's lofty peaks. During June, July, and August, when a truce has been called between the warring elements east and west of the range, the novice comes into his own. Then the high slopes are crossed and recrossed with the marks of ski and hiking parties, and powerful field glasses reveal the topmost pinnacle and the scarcely less lofty rim of Elliott Glacier to be black with spectators. Individual parties of a score or more, hundreds in the aggregate, have reached the top on a midsummer Sunday. The entire trip from Portland can be made between breakfast and supper.

The climber has the choice of two major routes: the

northeast and the south side. The novice will choose the south, since the northeast side is both exhausting and hazardous, chosen only by that strange breed of mountaineer who gains some inscrutable virtue by scaling a peak the hard way. A description of a typical round trip from Portland suggests the pattern followed by the Sunday climber.

Our hero gets up early on a beautiful summer morning, dresses in ordinary hiking clothes, and eats a hearty breakfast. If it is not a beautiful morning he stays in bed. Mount Hood is not to be trifled with, even in midsummer. He looks toward the peak, which is fifty miles eastward and in plain view from most residential sections of the city. If there is a tiny cloud suspended from the crest he takes another sweater along. That needlelike crest is eleven thousand feet higher than the point where he stands, and the tiny cloud suggests that it will most certainly be drafty up there.

He gets into his car and picks up his fellow climbers. He is one of a party because, if he doesn't already know it, he will be told at timber line that the beginner does not make the climb alone. All have similar equipment: ordinary hiking clothes, including heavy boots, preferably hobnailed— the sole concession to the nature of the outing. For comfort, each has dark glasses and grease paint in his pocket, and a substantial lunch.

The car heads east through the freshness and fragrance typical of summer mornings in the valley. In ten minutes it is out of the city, speeding past grove, orchard, and truck garden. It soons begins to mount through the foothills, and in fifty minutes more is at Government Camp, on the backbone of the range. Another ten minutes brings the party to

Timberline Lodge, where the car is parked among scores of others in the area facing the massive entrance.

Timberline Lodge is a million-dollar, two-and-a-half-story building of logs and native stone, erected by FWA during the "spend out of the depression" era, now supervised by the forest service and leased to private operators each season. Since costs were incidental in its planning and construction, it was built on a lavish scale, equipped with immense fireplaces, huge lounge rooms, sleeping accommodations, dining rooms, and other comforts dear to the novice but scorned by the hard-bitten mountaineer. Since this is the average summer week end, the vast lobby is crowded with skiers, tobogganers, and hikers. Early as it is, the first-aid station is already doing a rushing business, caring for the procession of sprains, bruises, and broken bones coming in a steady stream from the higher slopes.

Our party starts immediately for the heights. If they are completely without shame (in the eyes of the ever-sardonic veteran) or intent merely on gaining the summit via the quickest and easiest route, they take the ski lift, which swings them effortlessly up the first thousand feet. From that point on they are under their own power.

It is sheer, exhilarating fun at first. The mountain appears to hang almost vertically above them, vast and static. It seems as though a snowball could be tossed over the crest, though it is still two miles distant and almost a mile higher. From this height a vast panorama is already outspread below, and each upward step widens the view.

The first snow fields, interspersed with naked rock ridges, are soon left behind. The last skier and casual hiker dwindles on the slopes below. The sun is mounting with the party, and it is, strangely, hot and laborious going. And yet at each pause for rest—and these become increasingly sweeter—the wind has a new chill bite in it.

Now there is a huge moraine crumbling down from the base of the topmost cliffs. The party swings to the east and comes to the edge of an awesome chasm, floored with ice and walled on the farther side by a gleaming wall two thousand feet high. This is the cradle of White River Glacier, source of White River, a torrent which speeds eastward, far below.

Goggles and grease paint are put on here. From this point on the rock is sheathed in perpetual snow or ice. The party mounts on—wearily now, with the rest interval of more importance than the view—and comes to a cove at the head of the glacier where the air is momentarily foul with sulphur fumes issuing with the steam from cracks and crannies at the foot of the wall.

The final snow field extends from above the cove. At its top awaits the first and last real test of stamina: the 445-foot cliff guarding the summit. It is not a vertical wall, but so steep as to bar the amateur. Help is at hand, however, in the form of a three-inch manila rope snaking down from the heights. It has been moored there by the forest service early in the season, and lies in a groove already worn deep by the bodies of scores of climbers. The system is to grasp the rope firmly and walk up the groove. The descent is even simpler: wrap arms and legs around the rope and slide down.

Our party rests again, puffing in the thin air, before climbing the groove. The point at the foot of the rope might well be labeled "Cape Disappointment." More than one elderly couple have been forced to turn back here, less than five hundred feet short of the crest. Having lived within sight of the mountain all their lives, intending always to climb it, they have postponed the adventure too long. All their strength has been spent mounting this far; the last giant step is simply too much.

For persons of average stamina, however, it presents no great difficulty. Up the party goes in single file, clinging to the rope and resting perhaps three times on the way. They are now in the full force of the wind that scours the 11,000-foot level and feel like flies clinging to a wall. Laboriously they achieve the crest, come to their feet, and look about them, completely staggered. Being amateur mountain tamers, each had had a vague notion that a considerable expanse, comparatively level, awaited here. After all, a mountain has to have a top.

Instead there is a knife-edge ridge. They are standing on it, and the mountain immediately begins to descend on the other side. The highest point is at their right, along the ridge. Perched there is a sturdy cabin, anchored by cables to the hidden, solid rock. It is a forest service lookout cabin. Our party discovers, with a feeling of vague chagrin, that a forester lives there permanently throughout the summer, sweeping the horizon with powerful glasses, alert for a plume of smoke rising up from the several thousand square miles of timber outspread below him.

He is living there now. He appears at the door, beckoning to them cheerfully. He has been watching them climb and has hot tea ready for them—at ten cents a cup. The party threads the ridge in single file, leaning against the wind. At one point those subject to vertigo at great heights lower to hands and knees and crawl, unashamed. The ridge narrows

MOUNT HOOD

Mount Hood, Oregon, with its great open snow fields, is rapidly
gaining world renown for its unexcelled skiing. It is the most
accessible of the continent's lofty peaks

MOUNT HOOD
A ski trail in new snow leads to the wide-open spaces of Mount
Hood above Timberline

here to some six or eight feet. It seems narrower than a thread. At the right the side of the ridge falls away into the space above hidden Elliott Glacier. On the left, which is north, is an almost sheer drop of three thousand feet.

No tea tastes better than that prepared by the forester. The cabin sways ominously in the screaming wind, but their host assures them that it has withstood the fiercest winter gale. Having rested and regained their breath, the party goes out into the wind to enjoy the view.

It is a panorama far more impressive to our climber than when viewed from a luxurious seat in an airplane. Somehow he feels that he has earned this moment; unaided, by his own efforts, he has achieved the pinnacle.

And it seems, literally, like the top of the world. He has seen this glittering spire many times, from many angles, sometimes from a hundred miles distant; and it has never before occurred to him that the view from this topmost crag also covered those same immense distances. It is out-spread before him now, a complete 360-degree view of a major portion of the Pacific Northwest.

It includes almost half of the entire Cascades Range. Northward across the Columbia gorge—which is a mere fold in the lower hills from this high point—are the massive spires of Mounts Adams and St. Helens, the latter a perfect cone indented at the summit by its ancient crater. Still farther to the north, up the dwindling ridge, is mighty Rainier. The tip of remote Glacier Peak shows against the sky line.

To the south is the sharp spire of Mount Jefferson, the smallest of the ten giants of the range, a mere 10,495 feet in height. Its gleaming sides, fifty-odd miles distant, seem to be within rifle shot. More than seventy miles farther, beyond

Three-Fingered Jack and other lesser peaks, are the glittering spires of the Three Sisters, tiny above the curve of the earth.

Eastward the pine timber merges into the wheat land, and the black and golden squares of summer fallow and ripening grain encircle the Blue Mountains and merge into infinity. Southwest, west, and northwest is the ocean of green that blankets the Pacific slope. Half the standing timber of the nation is in Oregon and Washington, and more than half of that mighty stand is within view from Mount Hood's crest. Much has been said about the depletion of the forest, but to our climber it seems that there is enough left to furnish lumber to house the world. The Willamette Valley appears as a misty gash in the southwest. Here and there are lesser tilled valleys and individual patches of orchard and meadow. The Columbia meanders like a silvery ribbon westward. Otherwise the undulating green blanket seems unbroken. Actually, the forester explains, less than 20 per cent of the Pacific slope is under cultivation, after a century of settlement.

Thoroughly chilled, their joints beginning to stiffen, the party descends. It requires two hours to reach Timberline Lodge as opposed to the seven spent in the climb. Another hour and a quarter finds them back in Portland, in time for supper. Food never tasted better. To some members of the party the day's adventure is like a taste of heady wine; they will soon be members of the Mazamas, the Cascades' oldest alpine club. Each week end will find them sprinting for the peaks. Others will merely smile tolerantly, as one looks back at the errors of youth, and say with a comfortable sigh: "Well, sir, I've climbed my mountain."

Only the expert climbs the northeast side of Mount Hood alone. If he is not an expert he turns back—or fails to return. The novice joins a party of seasoned men and women— devotees of the "hard way"—and at first, fortunately, has no remote conception of the physical torture that lies ahead. At the moment it dawns upon him, usually after surmounting appalling Cooper's Spur, he is roped into the center of the column and it is then too late for the famous and sometimes pathetic speech beginning, "On second thought . . ." When he reaches the top he is a veteran.

It is called the Cooper's Spur route and begins at a forest camp high up on the northeastern slope, where the party has camped in preparation for an early morning start. To the innocent novice this jovial evening is a flattering interlude. He is among veterans, accepted as one of them. That there might be a sinister undercurrent in their affection—akin, for example, to that of cannibals dancing around their steaming pot, eying their portly visitor—does not intrude upon his grateful outlook.

In the chill light of dawn they emerge from the forest and begin the climb up the south rim of Elliott Glacier. At the top the novice yearns to ask: "Does it get any steeper than this?" The answer is Cooper's Spur, where they ascend to the 8500-foot level. The neophyte tries to gain sufficient breath to protest this manslaughter, but they are busy roping him into the line, smearing his face with grease paint, thrusting goggles upon him, and slapping his back with dismaying heartiness. Then the final exquisite torture begins.

The route now follows an incredible ridge, up a still steeper snow field, and so to the base of what appears to be a vertical cliff. The floundering novice peers up the cliff, clutching at hope. Somebody has made a mistake; a robust fly wouldn't attempt such a ghastly climb; they would have to turn back. But his captors gaily refer to this perpendicular mass as a "chimney" and start up it at once, clinging to a rope left dangling there by some unknown trail-blazing hobgoblins.

The rest of it remains vague in the novice's memory. He recalls vaguely that he made it to the top of the chimney, where cheerful voices assured him that the final cliff was only fifteen hundred feet high. He remembers placing his feet into steps hacked in the ice, and the tremendous effort required to raise his body to the next step, and so on up interminable steps. He recalls feet opposite his glazing eyes, and somebody breathing on his ankles: and the faint, pale, homicidal urge that stirred in him when some near-by maniac mentioned "the view."

At long last, when he comes to the first level footing he has seen in two vertical miles and has decided to collapse without shame or hope and permit himself to settle down in a boneless and effortless mass, and die on the spot, he finds that he has reached the top. For whatever it is worth, he is a veteran now: mostly, if not solely, because he has survived. . . .

And still our novice-veteran, being human, feels a faint stirring in his veins. Buddha-like, he crouches on that lofty crest, ostensibly enjoying the panorama into whose presence he has driven himself at such frightful cost. Actually he is looking down with mounting scorn and distaste at the long line of weaklings ascending toward him in calm and completely loathsome comfort, up the soft south side.

CHAPTER XIII

Roll Call of Giants

AMONG the ten major Cascades peaks whose crests approach or pass the two-mile level, Mounts Rainier and Hood are the frosting of the cake, as it were, in accessibility, development of playgrounds, and in popularity with the general public. More than half a million people live within two hours by motor from Hood's snow fields, and perhaps three quarters of a million within the same radius of Paradise Valley, on Rainier's lower ramparts. Of the million-odd tourists who permeate the Northwest during the normal summer season, those afflicted with "mountain fever" turn naturally to these adjacent slopes.

Yet the remaining eight giants of the range cannot properly be designated as "lesser" peaks solely because main streams of travel have passed them by. On the contrary, to a growing army of enthusiasts both in the Northwest and throughout the nation, the comparative isolation of some of the least-advertised pinnacles makes them all the more attractive. All have been scaled at one time or another, but a peak like Glacier, for example, has probably been surmounted by less than twoscore parties. Mount Washington was conquered less than two decades ago, after being labeled "impossible" during the preceding half century. Sinister Three-Fingered Jack—which is not even numbered among the first ten, since it thrusts a mere mile and a half skyward, resisted all attempts until its surrender to a climbing party in 1923.

The matter of inaccessibility alone is sometimes responsible for an individual mountain's popularity or lack of it, but not always. Why some of the Cascades' majestic peaks should remain unexplored and unknown except to the few is wholly inexplicable. A brief résumé of the ten—a roll call of giants, as it were—brings out some curious facts in that respect.

Let us begin at the northern end of the range, with Mount Baker. Here is a peak which dominates its horizon even more impressively than towering Rainier, since almost its entire mass rises up sheerly from its relatively low foundation. Its gleaming white dome, almost unmarred by naked cliffs, is a landmark far up in Canada, along the Straits of Juan de Fuca and from most points on Puget Sound. The Indians called it Komo Kulshan—"White Shining Mountain," or "White Watcher." To sailors beating down from Alaska or inbound from the Orient it was "White Friar," due to its fancied resemblance to the flowing robes of a Carmelite monk.

It is one of the Cascades' most beautiful peaks, and easily accessible. A highway skirts its base and mounts up to the crest of Kulshan Ridge, which joins Baker to Mount Shuksan, a scarcely less imposing peak hidden by Baker's bulk from the view westward. The lodge located here, plus a group of cabins, offers the usual accommodations. A ski lift carries the vacationist up to the higher slopes, above which beckon the eternal snow fields leading to the summit. Winter sports are popular enough, though its devotees are drawn largely from local communities.

And yet, to tens of thousands of people to whom Mount Baker is as much a part of their daily lives as the sunrise itself, it is something to be admired only from a distance. They see it from the cradle to the grave, but the vast rank and file never set foot on those familiar snow fields, never even mount to timber line. It never occurs to them to do so. In some indefinable way the resplendent peak is a symbol of beauty rather than the living reality. And, oddly enough, many local residents who have scaled Mount Baker have never again felt the same toward it; as though they had gained familiarity with—and thereby lost—an immaculate ideal.

No such aesthetic values or whims bar the way to Glacier Peak, the next in line, some sixty miles south of Baker. It is merely a rough, tough crag or series of close-group crags, surrounded by the most hostile terrain to be found in the Cascades. No highways go near it. Only an active man carrying his equipment on his back, or accompanied by an exceedingly mountain-wise pack horse, can scale the timbered ridges and savage, fog-hung gorges which bar the way to the lower slopes. Until some later era when the value of the timber outweighs the cost of blasting a way to it, or the chance discovery of a mineral deposit forces access to its solitude, Glacier will remain as truculently aloof as it was a century ago.

South of Rainier, which we have previously logged, Mounts Adams and St. Helens—two of the three, including

Hood, known as the "Guardian Peaks" of the Columbia—are fairly easy of access, yet overshadowed by the proximity of Rainier and Hood. St. Helens is an almost perfect cone, indented at the crest by its ancient crater. It is still regarded as a "live" volcano, though its last eruption occurred more than a century ago: a "blowup" more spectacular than damaging. A considerable area was covered with pumice cinders to a depth of ten to twenty feet, later solidifying into a hard-surfaced mass. Trees killed by this shower rotted in their places, leaving deep "tree wells" as a local oddity. Fragments of pumice littering the shores of adjacent Spirit Lake are lighter than water and will float several minutes before the honeycombed mass is saturated.

Spirit Lake is one of the numerous strange phenomena in the shadow of St. Helens. Indians believed the entire region to belong to the dead and to be the immediate residence of certain "devils" cast out from other tribes. Certainly the moans and shrieks which echo at intervals across the lake add color to this belief, though unimpressed scientists, as always, hasten to attribute these weird sounds to natural causes, such as the effect of the wind currents in the surrounding walls. The lake is a popular camp site during the season, particularly for many youth organizations.

The peak itself is not regularly climbed. Only occasional parties intent on adding another "big one" to their list scale its relatively smooth sides each season. Were it standing alone, it would be the Mecca for alpinists of the Northwest, but challenging Rainier is too close for the veteran and Hood is too attractive for the novice.

Mount Adams, second highest peak in the Cascades—12,307 feet—is also known only to the few. It stands in the center of the range about thirty miles north of the Columbia gorge and is flanked by lower ridges of rock which make access difficult. Yet it has many spectacular attributes which should one day make it a recreation area rivaling near-by Mount Hood.

Volcanic action has splashed Adams' snow line with yellow and vermilion crags. Seven distinct glaciers are outlined by black ridges, like giant claws clutching the peak. In this area are hot springs boiling up from some subterranean chaos, natural wells of pure carbon dioxide (when condensed, known as "dry ice"), and a deep ice cave into which the visitor descends via ladder to view glittering walls and odd lava formations by torchlight.

South of Mount Hood, some fifty miles, aloof and beautiful Mount Jefferson overlooks the high plateau for almost one hundred miles. It is accessible from both sides of the range, though no highway approaches its timber line, and in the field of mountain climbing has appeal only for the veteran. The novice may approach the base of the final spire, but only a handful of the expert alpinists have actually reached the top. Except for near-by Three-Fingered Jack, it is the Cascades' most difficult peak to conquer.

Close to the base of Mount Jefferson is a spectacle which, once viewed, is never forgotten. It is a natural park of several square miles in extent, sparsely forested with alpine fir and hemlock—themselves the most beautiful trees to be found in the Cascades—and blanketed with flowers and heavy turf. The whole expanse is jeweled with tiny lakes, some a few feet across, others covering several acres, their shores green with moss or radiant with blue lupine, crimson-tipped Indian paintbrush, or purple heather. The water is crystal-clear, and the bottom of each lake is solid rock, so that each has the appearance of a formal, tile-bottomed pool, though no human agency has contributed to the exquisitely beautiful effect. As though in an attempt to maintain this beauty in a barren land, the whole is irrigated by melting snow from Jefferson's vast slopes.

The wonder with which lovers of the outdoors have viewed this area is always tinged with regret. Only hundreds have seen it thus far. When the thousands come, as they inevitably will, the invariable marks of "popular" approval will be left behind: tin cans, rubbish heaps, abandoned but still smoldering campfires, and the scars left in the wake of uprooted shrubs.

The Three Sisters, each topping ten thousand feet, stand midway along the range between Mount Hood and Crater Lake. They are the last of the giants, and with the exception of Mount McLoughlin—which is actually the topmost crag in the series of ridges breaking down into the Siskiyous—are the final, perpetually snow-clad peaks in the southern end of the range.

The three peaks are closely grouped, with the South Sister a little aloof from the Middle and North Sisters, whose bases join. Though the south peak is even easier to scale than Mount Hood, and the Mackenzie Highway skirts the northern edge of the trio's common base, only a fraction of each season's novices choose the South Sister for their initial alpine adventure. The Middle and North Sisters are progressively more difficult to scale, the latter being a substantial test for the veteran.

It is the geologist who finds the Sisters area a happy hunting ground.[1] The whole region from the Columbia gorge south, and particularly the section of the range from Mount Jefferson to matchless Crater Lake, abounds in the record of thunderous, creative epochs when the world was young.

[1]See Chapter XVI.

CHAPTER XIV

Mountaineer Clubs

Many good-natured witticisms have been aimed at the inveterate mountain climber: the odd biped who never rides when he can walk, who never walks on the level when he can walk uphill, whose fetish is to take the longest, hardest, most dangerous way around—preferably in foul weather —to reach a given point.

He has a Jekyll and Hyde personality. For days on end he goes quietly about his business, pays his taxes, speaks kindly to his children, praises his wife's cooking, and helps old ladies across crowded intersections. He snores peacefully in his chair of evenings, during the fireside chat, and rouses at command to help Junior with his algebra. In a word, he is a normal, substantial Pillar of Society.

But come week end, he hurries home with a maniac gleam kindling in his eye and dives into his basement. When he emerges he has reverted to type. He is shambling, granite-jawed, his teeth clenched on an evil-smelling pipe. He drags strange gear behind him, which he tosses into his car. His wife—long since resigned, thankful only that the neighbors don't know and the insurance is paid up—stands shrinking on the side lines, holding the children close. "Yes, dears, that's your daddy. But remember him as he was, my precious lambs. Not—like this."

He disregards them; the trivialities of life are already forgotten. Other hairy-eared primates have joined him. They mutter, heads together, facing toward the mountains. One gestures to the southeast, another east; they compromise on the northeast, leap into the car, and are gone. Soon they are baying hopefully in the thinning timber; and presently, at long last, high up in the screaming crags, they revel in an orgy of chilblains, aching joints, freezing flesh, and deathly weariness—all the matchless and exquisite tortures that have haunted their dreams during the workaday week.

Nevertheless certain virtues accrue from this strange obsession. Over the years, however mouselike he may have been in the beginning, the veteran's character reflects his close contact with the mountains. When aroused, he is as inflexible as the iron peaks. This was demonstrated in the debate over the relative heights of Whitney and Rainier, and the far more bitter free-for-all that raged over the question of whether Rainier should or should not be named Tacoma. The scars of the latter battle, as in granite, remain unhealed.

But it is in defense of the mountains themselves that the addicts emulate Kipling's "thin red line of 'eroes." Along in the late twenties, in the golden predepression era, a company was formed to promote a cable lift to the summit of Mount Hood. Instantly it was as though a battered bugle sounded the alarm, and hidden drums began to roll.

The proposal was that a tramcar carrying a hundred passengers should run from Cloud Cap Inn on the east side of the mountain, beginning at an elevation of 6000 feet, and climb to Cooper's Spur, elevation 8500 feet. At this point a forty-foot tower would be erected, with cables carried to another tower, sixty feet high, fixed on the summit. Up this cable would glide a car carrying thirty passengers, to disembark them at the top; a grandstand view of the magnificent panorama of the Cascades and the two worlds divided by the barrier.

When this proposal was made public many people visioned the possibilities in publicity and tourist trade for the area, and became enthusiastic. Resort men, transportation men, hotel men, and others in similar lines who could be expected to benefit from the increased tourist trade applauded the plan.

Opposed to them were a relatively small group called the Mazamas, a mountaineering club.

The contest looked, at first glance, to be unequal. Money talks, and through this promotion scheme it spoke in commanding tones. But the Mazamas were accustomed to larger opponents. After an uproar that engaged the attention of the entire area, echoed in the halls of Congress, and brought out editorial comment in the *Saturday Evening Post*, the mountaineers won. The project was disapproved by the chief forester of the region—Mount Hood is situated in a national forest area—with the somewhat gallery-conscious but final words "Peaks like Hood, Shasta, and Whitney, preserved and revered as Nature made them, represent one of our greatest assets."

The promoters drew a last, weeping rabbit from the hat. They pointed to the thousands—nay, millions—of Americans too old, infirm, or busy to undertake the labor of climbing the mountain foot by foot, and who were as much entitled to a look at the view as other taxpayers who were quicker on their feet. These eyes that must remain forever empty of the view were scorned by the Mazamas, who asserted that anybody who couldn't climb a mountain—or wouldn't climb a mountain—didn't deserve to see the view.

"Mount Hood is a noble thing—clean, chaste, uplifting, ennobling—an inspiration, a classic creation too grand, too beautiful, too much a part of the better life of the people who look upon its lofty outlines to be despoiled by sordid commercialism."

When the flying adjectives had cleared away, and the project was dead, the question arose, "Just what or who are the Mazamas?"

The Mazama Club, it developed, is something exclusively born and bred on the Cascade Range, different from any other mountaineering club in the world and developed to fit the particular need of the peaks in which they take such truculent delight.

In the first place the Mazamas trace their parentage back to an outing club formed in 1883, when there was no mountain club on the continent except the Appalachian Mountain Club of Boston. But this outing club, it was said, quickly gathered too many members who wanted to sit by the fire and talk about mountaineering, rather than bundle up and actually lean against the crags. So in 1893 a few bold spirits decided to reorganize with new rules. The main rule would be that any applicant for membership must actually prove his or her ability and willingness to climb mountains. In other words, the applicant must have climbed a mountain.

The mountain cannot be a mere hillock but must appear on the accepted list. It must boast eternal snow, in the form of glaciers that never melt away, and there must be no other way of reaching the top than climbing on foot. To accentuate their new rule the prospective charter members of the new club agreed to meet on the top of Mount Hood to organize their club.

They did so, and the rule still stands. Thus automatically the "parlor athletes," the ladies who like those cute outdoor togs but in a cocktail environment, those seeking only entertainment, and the people who prefer to ride when they could and should walk, are eliminated by this preliminary rule.

This rule is the strictest of the club. Everything else is organized loosely, almost casually. Members joined the club from every community along the Cascades and presently grew in numbers and organized local clubs, so each mountain in the chain has some group near its base devoted to itself. Other members found their interests specific rather than general, and formed scientific clubs to study geology, vulcanology, minerals, botany, and what not. Still other groups, having climbed their mountain, felt they preferred a milder form of exercise and organized hiking clubs devoted to less austere levels.

Another group of supermen formed an exclusive and astoundingly hardy group called "Crag Rats," whose delight is to perform feats far above the average person's ability. All of these clubs, from one end of the Cascades to the other, are in a sense offshoots of the Mazama group, which goes along with six to nine hundred members, and a past membership totaling perhaps twenty thousand people, virtually all of whom have chosen Mount Hood for their qualifying climb or have included it among the peaks they scale, summer by summer, during their active years.

The Mazama Club members are officially or unofficially mixed with every movement designed to better the acquaintance of the public with the Cascade Mountains. So mountaineering practices in the Cascades have developed along informal lines that differ from the customs in any other mountain range in the country.

There are virtually no guides waiting to be hired to conduct parties up any of the mountains, with the exception of Mount Rainier, where six to a dozen professional alpinists are usually available to guide parties. Most of the thousands of climbers who ascend the peaks in a summer season are guided by Mazamas or ex-Mazamas who seem willing to go to any trouble to drag novices to the summit. Cynics have suggested that perhaps there is a dash of sadism in this generosity. Mazamas deny it, asserting that beginners do not suffer; they are merely enjoying a new experience.

Mount Hood is said to be the most climbed mountain in the United States, and perhaps in the world, with the exception of Fujiyama. On a single week end in summer there might be a dozen parties making the ascent, with several hundred people mingling at the top. One single party numbered four hundred. More than one season passed the two thousand mark. Climbs have been made in low shoes and summer clothes, with no more preparation than a bit of grease paint and a pair of goggles. At other seasons the mountain is terrible in its aspects and quick and sudden in the death it deals to unwary parties.

A traveler may climb the Matterhorn in the Swiss Alps.

He returns and says, "I climbed the Matterhorn," but he does not tell of the guides, perhaps two or three of them, who brought his equipment, dressed him, tied him to themselves with ropes, and told him where to set his feet. Anyone climbing the Cascades actually climbs the mountain himself. He brings his own equipment and plods along under his own power, relying on himself.

Some of the stiffest climbs on the continent are found in the Cascades. Usually there is an easy route up the mountain, such as Mount Hood's south slope, and since this is a favorite Sunday climb, a fixed rope is provided and steps are cut in the ice so that even the children and the aged may make the ascent. Similarly, on the north side route, a fixed rope is usually provided in preparation for a large party of novices. Nowhere else in the Cascades is a rope fixed. All other parties must climb without any outside aids. And the route may be so difficult that party after party of skilled men has been forced to turn back, or men may lose their lives attempting it.

The Mazamas scaled Mount Shuksan in 1906, the North Sister in 1910, and Three-Fingered Jack and Mount Washington in 1923, making the first known climbs of these peaks. The other Cascade peaks were conquered mostly in the fifties and sixties, prior to organized mountaineering effort. The club has a certain informal schedule. Each year they hold an annual outing of several weeks, in one area or another where they desire a closer acquaintance with the terrain. These outings are usually near some mountain peak, which may be climbed two or three times during the outing. No rules are laid down, but members of the party are expected to measure up to somewhat Spartan standards: to be co-operative, to swim in icy waters, sleep in sleeping bags on the ground, do a certain amount of hiking, look after themselves, avoid injuries that would discommode the party, and in general conduct themselves as if they loved the outdoors. Their thoughts, of course, are strictly their own.

Lists are open to the public. Anyone sponsored by a Mazama or claiming acquaintance with members of the party is welcomed. So with each affair staged by the club. No membership ticket is required for anyone sharing their climbs, their "local walks," or their ascent of this or that peak. A love of the outdoors makes anyone welcome, especially if the visitor has self-reliance and a little common sense. The organization of the club is the despair of professional organizers, who cannot get a grasp of the framework to identify it. But somehow, like timber wolves, the Mazamas know their own.

Over the years the Mazama Club—predating the forest service and other conservation groups—has added much to the understanding and appreciation of the Cascades.

Members of this club were responsible for the creation and preservation of Crater Lake National Park. They have consistently influenced forest conservation, good roads, study of trees and birds; they keep records on the glaciation of peaks, and among them are members who are authorities on certain aspects of geology. Any scientific party wanting a guide to any part of the Cascades area can find his man among the Mazamas, and in addition will find him delighted to offer his services free.

Certain peaks, such as Mount Hood, closely circled by a good motor highway, with well-equipped public inns perched high on the slopes, are developed for summer and winter sports with the full consent of the Mazamas. In fact from this group there is organized a "rescue committee" which spends its week ends on the ski slopes of Mount Hood, ostensibly to ski, but actually to carry down the injured from among the thousands of amateurs and half-skilled skiers swarming the slopes on a winter week end. Other peaks, such as Glacier Peak, austere, forbidding, usually swathed in clouds, and virtually unknown even to the residents of the area, will remain a wilderness if the Mazamas have their way.

Down the backbone of the range, with the approval and part-time help of the Mazamas, there is being constructed a "skyline trail." Originally open to pack horses, then in part to automobiles, it will someday accommodate motor travel along the length of the range, from the gloomy base of Glacier Peak down the range to Crater Lake, a magnificent drive of perhaps four hundred miles.

CHAPTER XV

Death on the Mountain

On a clear day the crest of Mount Hood seems to be within rifle shot of Timberline Lodge. Actually it is three and seven tenths miles. The distance seems puny, but should one be on or near the summit when a sudden storm breaks, the return trip may be as formidable as the space between stars.

Late in March 1938 a party left Timberline Lodge to make the climb. It was Sunday morning, the sun shining on new, deep snow. The way to the top was in sight, though the sky eastward was threatening. Each member of the party was experienced, confident, and in good physical shape. Some were on skis, some on snowshoes.

Cold was intense at the higher altitudes, and a strong wind seemed to grow stronger. A fine sleet blew near the top, depositing ice on the goggles and faces of the climbers. The going was bad. Had there been a weakling in the party —if each man hadn't been top-notch in his skill, hardihood, and pride—somebody would have said, "I can't go any farther"—and tragedy would have been averted. As it was, they pushed on for fully an hour after every tenet of caution had been broken.

They left skis and snowshoes at Crater Rock and began the ascent of the final cliff short of the summit. The wind clutched at them and the sleet grew worse. They became sheathed with ice. If they took off their goggles to clean them their eyelids froze together.

Suddenly Roy Varney pitched forward into the snow. They thought he had fainted from exhaustion. Actually his clothing was not quite heavy enough for the punishing wind, and the vitality had been draining from his body. Suddenly alarmed, they turned back, short of the summit, and hurried down to their skis and snowshoes.

Varney must now be carried and they had no equipment for carrying him. They lashed him on skis, but the sleet had changed to snow which trailed from each ridge in deepening drifts. To flounder through the feathery mass with a heavy body was next to impossible; even those on snowshoes sank to the knees. The skiers decided to go down for help, leaving two of the snowshoers with Varney. They followed along slowly, trying to drag him, while the eternal wind sucked at their strength.

Timberline Lodge was in view of the skiers, but the storm was following them down. They descended in long zigzags. Those dragging Varney of necessity came more slowly, and the storm descended to and past them. The skiers stayed together to within the last mile of Timberline, then each chose his own path on the final sprint.

At Timberline they asked for the "snow cat," a rescue outfit powered by a rugged crawler-type tractor. But the operator was down in Portland and had the keys with him, so nobody could start the "cat." The skiers themselves were too exhausted to return up the mountain. They telephoned to Government Camp, and a rescue party was immediately formed and came slogging up to Timberline. This required more than an hour. The storm was now full-grown, blotting out everything above Timberline.

Meanwhile the men with Varney were exhausted. Varney seemed to be dead. If they stayed with the body the storm would engulf them. It was of blizzard proportions, screaming across the unprotected snow field. It was impossible to drag or carry the dead man farther. They left him there and fought their way down to Timberline.

This act was later held against them. Some held that Varney died after being abandoned. Others were convinced that Varney had died earlier in the battle and the two snow-shoers would have perished with him had they stayed with the body. In any case the exhausted pair insisted on returning with the rescue party, and they found Varney dead.

The tragic episode seemed over. The principals returned to Portland, broke the news to Varney's family, discussed events among themselves, and finally fell into beds in their various homes.

Next morning a phone call came to the leader. A certain young man, Gueffroy, hadn't reported to work. His employers were calling. Hadn't Gueffroy been in the party? Was he injured or sick? The leader checked with a few of the others and found that Gueffroy had been among the skiers who had swooped down on Timberline in advance of the storm. The inn had been in plain sight. Each of the skiers had followed his favorite slope down on the homestretch. In the excitement nobody had noticed whether or not he had reached the inn.

The leader phoned Timberline Lodge and asked somebody to look in the parking lot. Sure enough, Gueffroy's car was there, half buried in snow. This was Monday morning. The storm had blown over, and it seemed incredible that any human being could have survived the night on the snow field. Nevertheless he must be looked for at once.

The usual rescue procedure—inspiring and spontaneous, yet carefully supervised—was carried out. The leader stays constantly at the telephone, directing the ever-widening campaign. Volunteers on snowshoes and skis work up through the thinning timber. Equipment and clothing may be commandeered from any person having a surplus or gathered up from sporting goods stores. The full facilities of the lodge, Government Camp, the telephone, the bus, or anybody's car are at the service of the rescue party. Women keep fires roaring and the coffee hot, and volunteers by the hundreds spread out along the lower slopes, with new recruits hurrying from all points of the compass. Time is of the essence, and as the hours pass newspapers and radio give increasing time and space to the effort.

Experienced lieutenants direct the actual search, making sure that each gully and ravine is checked. Men who know the mountains winter and summer, who understand the slopes that appear so innocent on a clear day but betray staggering feet when storm and darkness blot out all landmarks, relive the scene through the eyes of the lost one and try to decide which of the dimming, howling ridges had diverted him from the true course. Probable areas are combed first, then the possible, then the improbable and remote. New, deep snow makes the task infinitely more difficult. Any drifted mound, bush, or boulder might be the body they seek.

After Tuesday night had come and gone the search was for Gueffroy's body. Nobody expected to find him alive. Sometimes the body is never found, depending on the whim of season and storm. By this time the search was grim and dogged, with hundreds of volunteers close to exhaustion.

They found Gueffroy's skis stuck upright in the snow, within easy distance of Timberline Lodge. Why, nobody knows. Strange fancies, plausible and pleasant, whisper in the ear of a man skirting the extreme outer threshold of exhaustion and cold. His body would be within walking distance, so they combed the adjacent terrain. Instinct alone should have carried him on toward the lodge, which must still have been in plain view, even to dimming eyes. There was no slightest trace of him on that route. The storm could have swept him into an adjacent gully, but the gully was empty. He was somewhere near by, hidden under drifts within view of his abandoned skis; but where?

Finally they returned to the skis and dug down through the snow to his footprints. It required expert, laborious work, but step by step they uncovered the trail. Each wavering change of direction sent another party to scour the indicated terrain, but they were always disappointed. At last the trail led into the timber; and they found him there, seated under a tree, snow-whitened but in comfortable pose, as though he had sat down to rest not long before. His attitude showed plainly that he had been exhausted by his climb and struggle. Something in his pose seemed to protest that he wasn't lost; he knew where he was, where he was going. It was only a short distance down to the shelter of the timber. He was practically in the clear; and wasn't a bone-weary man entitled to sit down to rest a moment before going on?

Thus he had fallen into the longest sleep, dreaming, no doubt, that he was safe at home, reading in the papers about a storm in the mountains and a man named Varney, not Gueffroy, who was lost in the bitter peaks. "Better get out there and give them a hand," he may have thought drowsily. "He'll be tired. And cold."

CHAPTER XVI

Geology of the Cascades

To MANY an outdoor specialist, mountains are worth while only in relation to a particular interest or hobby. The fisherman finds nothing of promise above timber line. To the crag rat the terrain below the snow fields is merely ground to be covered. The timberman appraises the fisherman's prize creek as an obstacle to logging, looks upon the fisherman himself as a potential breeder of forest fires, and assumes the alpinist to be a completely harmless dimwit afflicted with an uncontrollable urge to throw handsprings among the Shasta daisies and sing, "Hark! Hark! The Lark!" To the ski addict a naked rock ridge projecting from the snow is an unpleasant object, something to hurry by.

Happy indeed is the man whose outlook embraces a variety of interests rooted in a great mountain range. To him there are many vistas and dimensions hidden from the specialist. Each excursion to the heights is a many-sided adventure; a well-rounded banquet, as it were, instead of a single course of canapés, squab, or beefsteak.

To such a gourmet the geology of the Cascades is a fascinating chapter whose drama never fades and whose interest-gripping possibilities approach the infinite. It is no mere study of lifeless rock but an outspread record of thunderous forces in conflict when the world was young. No formal scientific background is necessary to enable the amateur to read the signs and interpret the clues. Brief research is sufficient. Thereafter he no longer wanders at random through a chaos of unrelated dimensions. Each ridge, peak, and canyon finds its proper place, like the pieces of a jigsaw puzzle merging together, and he is touring the static and stately ruins of a bygone age.

Fifty million or so years ago—so the story is revealed—the Pacific Ocean lapped the western slopes of the Rocky Mountains, and the entire Oregon Territory lay quiet under the waves. Great creative forces thrust up the barrier now known as the Cascades and blocked off this inland area from the ocean. This landlocked sea changed gradually into a fresh-water region clothed with tropic vegetation. Huge mammals of the prehistoric era roamed the jungles. The dinosaur and giant sloth fed and rested on its shores, and laid their bones in beds of ooze which later changed to rock and can be seen today.

Here, under palms and sequoias, the saber-toothed tiger—most formidable feline of all time—pursued the tiny three-toed horse and may have aided that creature's evolution into the swift animal we know today. Here are fossil evidences of the twelve-inch deer, the early species of camel and rhinoceros, and a primeval elephant. Here, too, dwelt the unique Oreodon, an insatiable creature the size of a coyote, with a set of teeth adapted for both grazing and meat eating, and ugly tusks which unquestionably haunted the dreams of prehistoric man.

Evidence is found to support the belief that animals not now native to this continent once dwelt here, and perhaps originated here, to cross an ancient land bridge to Asia to survive the glacial age in some different spot. Some dreamers go so far as to imagine this quiet inland lake as the cradle of all human life.

Meanwhile the terrific heat and pressure that raised the Cascades vented itself in successive lava flows, bursting out through live volcanoes along the backbone of the ridge and flooding eastward over the inland lake. Above these lava flows new lakes formed, and new vegetation grew and died in successive ages, only to be covered again by another boiling flood. The Cascades were already cutting off the warm winds of the Pacific from this inland area, and the glaciers from the north slipped down to scour the slopes and carry their loads of gravel to the valleys. And again the lava burst out and the level of the plateau was built a few hundred feet higher.

When all was quiet, and the scene was much as it is today, other great forces erupted beneath the lava, and thrust great cliffs two thousand feet into the open, bringing up the hidden layers which were thousands of feet under the surface before the crust broke. In these cliffs the story can literally be read today, and this glimpse into the past makes the area one of the most interesting perhaps in the world.

Much of the ancient story can be studied in the sheer walls of the Columbia gorge. The river is recognized as antecedent to the rise of the Cascades, and apparently fought its way through the rising barrier as the barrier rose, keeping its way open to the sea. The story repeats itself in the Picture Gorge of the John Day Valley, and the Abert and

Summer Lake rims reveal mammal graveyards of millions of years ago. Over all the inland plateau the old and new lava flows can be traced. Where the Mackenzie Highway climbs the Cascade barrier, just north of the Three Sisters, the most "recent" lava flow, perhaps only a few hundred years old, lies naked of vegetation, as new and untarnished as if only yesterday some giant dumpcart flung the rocks in disorderly heaps by the roadside.

A thousand local "wonders" are common in this area. A "lava cave" or fold in the rock may lead the tourist a mile underground from the level plain. Ice caves are chill on the hottest day. During a blizzard a sheepherder will drive his flock toward an opening in the ground and find a sloping, shallow shelter that houses himself and the sheep from the weather. The city of Bend once disposed of its sewage by the simple method of boring down to an underground cave and directing the sewers to that receptacle. "Cinder buttes" or dead volcanoes rise abruptly hundreds of feet from the flat surface. The "rimrocks" are vast level stretches of rock against the sky, with the valleys scooped out below them. Fossilized wood sinks in water, while the pumice stone floats; and a wealth of semiprecious stones, deposits, and glasslike rocks of odd colors and patterns bear witness that the white-hot furnace of creation once worked here.

Into the cracks and faults of the laboring rocks were deposited a treasure of gold, which miners along both sides of the Cascades pan out today as it is loosened and washed down the streams. In their shacks at night the miners tell each other of the mythical river Oregon, which, they claim, once drained the inland lake, flowing traversely across the southern Cascades in a deep V-shaped trench, which in time became filled with gold. The bed is long since leveled off by slides and shiftings of soil, and great trees grow over the ancient watercourse, but under it all lies the treasure. Many a miner, obsessed with the dream of the river Oregon, has spent his years excavating for this old river bed. The Rogue River, tumbling down from the southern Cascades to the sea, is panned each summer by miners along its shoals and sand bars, and each winter flood renews the treasure. Old-timers assert that the Rogue crosses the ancient bed of the river Oregon, renewing its gold deposits yearly from that vast treasure house.

While this creative activity was building up the eastward side of the Cascades the western side was hammered by the surf of the Pacific Ocean. Then another fold of the ocean bed rose a hundred miles or so to the west of the Cascades, to form a low range that cut off the ocean again and made another inland sea or lake. The bed of this lake was built up by silt and glacial deposits to the present-day coastal valleys, which are only a little above sea level. The coast range failed to rise above the sea in the extreme north, and we have the Puget Sound area, still submerged. The Olympic Range, to the west of Puget Sound, is regarded as part of the coast range, and the hundreds of islands in the San Juan group are supposed to be the tops of mountains still submerged. Vancouver Island takes its place in this picture as the top of a cluster of these same hills, and here, too, it is common to find the ancient sea shells high on the rocky slopes, lying in deposits so large that they must have been laid down when the spot was under water.

Reading the history of the area in the rocks and soils, the students of the prehistoric say that the coastal strip is much more recent in development than the area east of the Cascades, where the inland lake once lay shimmering. The lake newly formed by the coast hills in turn drained away, mostly through the Willamette River, which joins the Columbia about a hundred miles above its mouth. The glacial age sent sheets of ice down to scour these new valleys, and left evidences in the curious mounds of earth near Tenino, in the state of Washington, in the barren gravel and sand of the Chehalis Valley, and the huge boulders in the Eola Hills of the Willamette Valley, supposedly carried from their distant source by floating cakes of ice, and dropped into the silt as the ice melted. Other signs and evidences are numerous in the low valleys, and the whole area is a rich ground for fossil hunters.

Three "lost mountains" persist in the geological view of the Cascades. Far to the north "Mount Si" once thrust its hoary head into the upper air, but during the mountain-building era this peak was covered by newer volcanic formations. From time to time the region is shocked by the tremendous jar and momentary shudder of an earthquake. This is taken to mean that old Mount Si is shaking at his coverlet, impatient with the newer rocks that keep him hidden.

In the southern half of the Cascades, where the Three Sisters are grouped, and the adjacent lower peaks are known as "Husband," "Brother," and other names taken from a family relationship, the eye of the imagination sees a picture that once was familiar in the region. A mountain rests on these various family peaks, each one received intimately into its base, and above them the bulk of the mountain thrusting up thousands of feet above them. Since the remaining bits of this mountain are able to top ten thousand feet, the old-

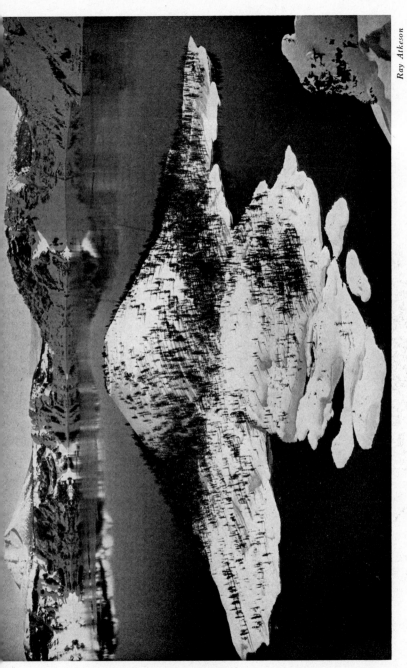

A snow-white jewel floating on the mile-high turquoise of Crater Lake. Wizard Island with its volcanic slopes draped in snow, viewed from the northwest rim of the lake, is a scene indescribable in beauty

Ray Atkeson

MOUNT ST. HELEN'S TO SPIRIT LAKE, WASHINGTON

time "Mount Multnomah," as traced by the geologists, must have been a tremendous peak indeed.

Still another mountain, "Mount Mazama," rises, in the eye of imagination, at the southern end of the Cascades, where Crater Lake's deep-sunk pool of blue lies two thousand feet below the rim of an old crater. The geologists here re-create the outline of Mount Mazama, rearing up far above the crest of the range, and no doubt rumbling and smoking for centuries before the cataclysm occurred that removed the peak, opened a crater, and made way for the lake. Here the story would be easier to tell if the geologists were in complete agreement on whether the top of Mount Mazama blew off and scattered eastward—or somehow sunk inside the mountain in a vast cave-in of material, to fill some inner vacuum. Whatever the facts—and the pages are blurred here —the "death" of Mount Mazama still persists in Indian legend.

Most of the notable research into the prehistoric story of the world has been done by scientific parties, headed by a trained scientist. In the Cascades area, where men had to use the tools that came to hand, the searching parties were sheepherders wearing out their lonely hours on the slopes of the Cascades, cowhands riding the range, army troops dodging the Indian snipers, and even the Indians themselves. All were earnest in their efforts to bring in specimens, not to a trained scientist but to a little Irish minister who pointed his congregation to the future while he turned yearning looks backward into the far reaches of the past.

Thomas Condon, pioneer geologist of the Cascade region, brought to the attention of the scientific world the peculiar geology of this region, where the past lies like an open book for all to read. His collection of specimens is unparalleled. His imaginative description of the prehistoric Cascade country reads like a fairy tale, soundly based on fact, and his absorbing interest in every rock and fossil has made the entire country conscious of the wealth of geologic history.

Condon was born in southern Ireland in 1822. His family brought him to America when he was eleven, and settled on a farm which is now Central Park in New York City. His education was gained through work rather than academic study. A florist taught him to love flowers and their origins, while he earned his living as a handy boy there. A kindly neighbor gave him lessons in drawing that served him well later. A physician engaged him as office boy and made him familiar with the methods of science. He developed his critical faculties in a debating society and began to collect his own fossils as a by-product of his walks to teach a country school. He turned his thoughts to the ministry, managed to work his way through a theological institute, offered himself as a volunteer in the mission field, and was sent to the Cascades area.

This was in 1852. With his young wife, Condon, now thirty years of age, set sail in a clipper ship from New York around Cape Horn to the Oregon Territory. He reached Portland and was assigned to a near-by church. His energy far outran the needs of the self-sufficient and perhaps somewhat smug pioneer families in the Willamette Valley, and he yearned for a richer harvest of souls to be garnered in the outposts across the Cascade Range. The spot he chose was The Dalles, then a wild and unpredictable town where the reckless spirits of the great inland basin gathered to spend their gold, sell their stock, drink, and dispute. Here were steamboat men, gamblers running twenty-four hours a day to entertain the gold-laden miners, military detachments whose joy was hunting Indians, and plenty of the swift and stealthy native sons of the high plateau.

Condon moved to The Dalles. He had scarcely an adequate church, and no study in which to compose his sermons. So he paced the hills, jotting down notes for his Sunday service. The terrain here is dry, barren, rocky, and stupendous in its wild elemental upthrust of pinnacle, cliff, and lava formation. There was little vegetation to hide the bare bones of the earth, and Condon, as usual, gathered up what he saw about him. It wasn't long before a hammer and pick became part of his equipment on these walks. When he opened a section of rock and found inside it a miraculously preserved leaf impression of some shrub that grew long before the Pyramids were planned, he became obsessed with an excitement he could scarcely control. Every moment he could spare was spent out among the rocks. He traced with wondering eyes the record of lava flow upon lava flow that built up the plateau. He became fascinated with the cliffs above the river, where the Columbia cuts through the mountain range, cleaving it from crest to sea level.

Between the flows of lava Condon saw the long ages which reduced the rocks into soil and deepened the soil until plants, then shrubs, then trees could grow. Then above the ages of growth came another lava flow, and the same story of weathering and growth and decay before another layer of lava covered it. He found fossil remains of prehistoric animals in these deeply laid strata, one or two thousand feet below the rim of the gorge, and under perhaps a dozen of these successive flows. He gathered the fossils, tremendously impressed, and carried them home to place in his "collection." It soon became customary for parties of travelers, lying over between steamboat runs, to visit Condon and discuss his collection. He was physically active and could lead parties out to see the rocks and up across the wild area at the base of Mount Adams, where he pointed out the successive terraces laid by successive lava flows. He explained, with Irish ingenuity and colorful words, the mystery of the deep ice caves below the rocks, and told his story in such simple language that even the active and reckless men who swarmed the city of The Dalles paused to listen. And each in turn located new rocks and specimens and brought them into The Dalles to be explained by the minister.

So the rocks poured in, carried by miner, soldier, and sheepherder. In 1864 one Captain Drake made camp near the Crooked River, a snow-fed stream rising on the eastern slopes of the Cascades to cut a gash three hundred feet deep across the plateau. The captain set out with part of his men to chase a few Indians. When he returned he found his camp "a vast geological cabinet. Everybody has been gathering rocks." The specimens contained fossil shells, which the captain was loath to believe were marine shells, since the 5000-foot barrier of the Cascades separated the area from the seaward valleys, but he sent them down to Condon with the next supply train, complaining of their vast weight but adding "a few specimens I picked up myself."

This gave Condon an inkling of what might wait for him

on the high plateau outside of The Dalles, and drove him near a scientific frenzy. There was no way to visit the country except in the company of the soldiers, since the inland Indians were far from subdued. So he commissioned soldiers and miners and trappers and anyone else who ventured into the inland area to bring him more rocks. The Dalles at that time, in the 1860s, was a boiling center of steamboat travel, and the accident of schedules made all passengers wait overnight there before continuing upstream to connect with the transcontinental stage lines (and later the railroads) or downstream on their way to the growing city of Portland, where they might take ship to any part of the world. The custom of visiting Condon's collection became a regular part of the trip. Among the hundreds and thousands of visitors were scientists. Condon was soon in touch with the Smithsonian Institution, shipping specimens and receiving in exchange the newest scientific bulletins they forwarded. So he received his first copy of Darwin's great work on the origin of species and so he learned that his fossils of leaf and plant and mammal were actually adding a new chapter to the story of the past. One little new member of the horse family was given Condon's own name as discoverer.

Wider and wider grew his correspondence, and he infused his collecting enthusiasm into anyone he could find who was setting off across the great untouched country. His fame by this time was spreading, so scientists made the arduous trip across the continent to see him and his collection, and to hear his own sparkling redramatization of the creation of the Cascade country.

Soon Condon was giving lectures in geology about the state between Sundays, and occasionally missing a Sunday in his pulpit. He performed the miracle of packing the hall with young people who ordinarily would have had no interest whatever in the dawn of creation. However, his scientific interest in no way detracted from his firm belief in the doctrines of religion. He maintained that the Bible was given as a revelation of spiritual truths, rather than scientific truths, and the common doubts of the time concerning the authority of the Word passed over his head.

It presently became apparent to everyone, and finally to himself, that his duty to humanity lay along the path of science and teaching, rather than the ministry, and his church reluctantly released him to the faculty of Pacific University, a pioneer college at Forest Grove. From this quiet seat of learning he moved on to the young University of Oregon at Eugene, and until his death he taught and collected and classified. From his teaching is derived much of the interest in geology about the area. His collections approach the dimensions of scientific treasures. His studies of the Cascades blazed the trail for present-day research. He died around the turn of the century, and lies buried in sight of the Cascades he loved.

CHAPTER XVII

Crater Lake

ON ANY STANDARD LIST of the continent's "natural wonders of the world" the name of Crater Lake will be found near the top. On the geologist's handbook it is rated as number one. Many aspects of it appear to defy accepted natural laws.

It is located at the crest of the Cascades, near its southern end: a body of water of incredible blueness, lying more than two thousand feet down inside an ancient crater, and walled in by sheer cliffs. It can be approached only by descending a man-made path that angles down the steep cliffs inside the rim; or by scrambling down a dangerously steep wall that requires mountaineering skill for safe passage.

From the surface of the water Wizard Island projects eight hundred feet, clothed with evergreens. Another rock, the "Phantom Ship," seems from some angles, particularly at dusk, to be a ship in full sail. The lake is two thousand feet deep at the deepest part. It is the largest lake of its kind in the world, with no close competitors.

Most visitors find their enjoyment in a quiet contemplation of this blue lake that lies far below their feet, but geologists turn immediately to the riddle of its creation, as suggested by the rocks and terrain.

Contours of the area suggest that once a mighty mountain rose above the Cascades at this place, the highest in the line of marching white peaks. It towered perhaps a mile and a half above the backbone of the ridge, which here is about eight thousand feet in elevation. This mountain is so real in the minds of geologists that it is named Mount Mazama, and usually any reference to the white peaks of the Cascade range includes Mount Mazama as if it still rose in its place. It was an active volcano, flooding the land to the east with lava and helping to build up the high plateau that lies eastward of the Cascade Range. From its mighty glaciers flowed a mighty river, westward to the sea, cutting deep canyons and forcing its way through the intervening coast hills. These canyons now permit the Rogue River to flow along their bottoms, draining this part of the Cascades. The Rogue is a tremendously important stream, but apparently is only a trickle compared with the flow of the river that once derived from the long-lost slopes of old Mount Mazama.

Some cosmic upheaval that can only be imagined removed the top of the mountain and opened a hole four thousand feet down inside of it.

One theory holds that the top blew off in a tremendous explosion, and the inside boiled out to leave the crater empty. But there is little evidence of a recent flow of such proportions. The marks of ancient glaciers that once slid down the slopes of the peak are still evident, not covered by lava. Any such venting of perhaps seventeen square miles of molten rock must certainly have left its mark on the countryside. This difficulty aids the alternate theory that the top of Mount Mazama fell inside the mountain, but the suggestion is as hard to swallow as the mass of rock would have been. So the first mystery of Crater Lake is "Where did the inside of the mountain go?"

There is more. The level of the lake is constant, yet it receives the winter precipitation of nine to fifteen feet of water a year and has no outlet that can be discovered. The water is perfectly fresh, not salt as it should be if the level of the lake were maintained by evaporation. The surface, although six thousand feet above sea level, never freezes. This mystery may be capable of explanation, but the explanation is not common property.

The blue of the water is another mystery. It is blue on bright days, as other lakes are, but when the sky is overcast it retains and even strengthens its blue. Other lakes as high, as pure, as walled in by cliffs, do not have this property of blueness. It seems a peculiar possession of Crater Lake. The color persists as the visitor descends the thousand-foot path inside the rim and leans down to dip his hand into the water, to see if it is colored with some artificial dye. Then he finds that the water is actually so clear that the print of a newspaper can be read when it is fifteen feet below the surface. And still the water at his feet is blue.

The existence of Crater Lake has been known to Indian tribes for many centuries, but it was not reported to white men, since the lake was both a sacred high place and a place of danger. The first reported discovery was made in 1853, as part of a lively episode typical of the pioneer West.

The gold camp at Jacksonville on the Rogue River in southern Oregon was the center for rich diggings along the seaward slopes of the Cascades and down the richly auriferous gravel of the Rogue itself. The creeks were laden with gold, new claims were profitable, and the gold fever, with gambling and gunplay, kept the tension high. Into Jacksonville came a party of prospectors from California. They bought a few supplies and refused to discuss their plans. Rumors grew that they sought a certain "Lost Cabin" claim reputed to be fabulously rich and located up some obscure branch of the Rogue. When the party left camp, stealing out in the darkness, they were followed by a party of Oregon men who were determined, in the phrasing of the day, to "help" the California men find the claim, and so share in the discovery.

The Californians soon became aware of pursuit, and a grim game of hide-and-seek took place in the steep canyons, among the almost impenetrable underbrush, until both parties used the last of their supplies, became aware that they were lost, and faced starvation.

In their extremity the Oregon leader, one John Hillman, proposed that they join forces to save their lives. As leader of the combined party, he found his job difficult. Game was scarce, and all the hills looked alike. They must find Jacksonville, or they would wander in the wilderness until they were all dead. It was necessary to climb some peak of the near-by Cascades to fix directions.

In the ascent to what he hoped would be a sufficiently high point, Hillman was riding a pack animal and watching on all sides for game. The sparse alpine timber gave way to a mountain meadow and he thought he saw a deer. He watched intently to one side, while the animal chose its own path.

The mule stopped short. Spread out at his feet, fifteen hundred feet below him, was the great blue lake. If he had been riding a blind mule, Hillman said, he would have fallen over the cliff.

He summoned the rest of the party, and they forgot their hunger in the marvel before them. They spent several hours circling the lake and voting on a name, which they wrote on paper and placed in a split stick to mark their discovery.

They found their way back to Jacksonville (without the Lost Cabin claim) but by this time had lost their bearings with regard to the lake, and since one may ride within a few yards of the edge without suspecting its existence, the astounding "Blue Lake" passed into the category of miners' tales and was forgotten.

This left the way open for another "discovery" in 1862, when a party of prospectors, traveling south along the broad top of the ridge, came out in a meadow adjoining the lake and found the water they sought for their camp lying deep in the crater. They, too, spent some time trying to find a way down to the lake. When they rolled a few rocks over the edge they got some idea of the height of the encircling cliffs and decided to melt snow instead of dipping up the water. They named the lake "Deep Blue Lake" and returned home with an approximate idea of its location.

In 1865 the lake was discovered by three different parties, hunting game or Indians, with each party believing itself the first to look upon the astounding view. Their descriptions partook of the hysterical, and little credence was given them. Finally the stories were told at Fort Klamath, on the eastern side of the Cascades, and officers of the fort made up a party to visit the lake. This was the first visit that was not rated a new discovery. Actually each person who sees Crater Lake for the first time feels the emotions of an original discoverer. However vivid the description, whatever pictures he has seen, he is unprepared for the astounding reality.

A rough road was opened into the lake in 1869, and a boat carried down to the water. Meanwhile a boy was born in Ohio, by name William Gladstone Steel, who was to find his destiny linked with the future of Crater Lake. He carried his lunch to school wrapped in newspaper. Reading this scrap while he lunched, he learned of the blue lake deep in a mountain crater in Oregon, a land he knew very little about. He determined to visit the lake someday. His family moved to Oregon in 1869, but the fifteen-year-old lad was thirty years old before he looked down on the lake, since the area was hundreds of miles from the settlement in the Willamette Valley. Few people had seen it, and many actually questioned its existence. Then he made the trip, saw the lake, and realized that now he had a purpose in life. The lake must become a national treasure.

It seems odd now that such a project should meet organized opposition, but it took seventeen years of uphill work before Steel found enough support for his project to win favorable action in Congress. Commercial interests were already gobbling up the vast forests, draining lakes, dredging fertile bottom land into rubble to find gold, and fixing private ownership tags on water sources that might have served a countryside. It was the era of individual exploitation, believed at the time to be the natural order of development in a new country. It would have been possible for a group of families, or one large family, to stake a claim to

Crater Lake and encircle its marvels in the chains of private ownership.

However, Steel made a dogged fight. President Cleveland, always responsive to appeals to save the natural wealth of the country, and Theodore Roosevelt, who knew the shortest way through a maze of red tape, listened sympathetically to Steel, and in the end the area was set aside as a national park. Protected by the Department of the Interior, Crater Lake will be treated as a scenic treasure. Every provision is made for the comfort of the traveling public. Otherwise the area is retained in a primitive state, much as it was before the white men came to the Cascade country.

The national park was established in 1902, with an area of 249 square miles. Forested areas alternate with mountain meadows carpeted with grass and wild flowers. The lake itself is the central attraction, but its position at the crest of the Cascades permits the visitor to view many thousand square miles of the seaward side and the contrasting range land to the east. From the public inn and other housing units grouped at the western edge of the rim, the visitor may take short or long walks to near-by canyons, waterfalls, peaks, surface lakes, and other scenic spots. Bird and animal life is protected. A "rim road," thirty miles long, circles the crater and offers a variety of views of the lake lying far below.

No fish were found in Crater Lake at the time of its discovery. They were planted by Steel in 1888. He carried minnows from the Rogue River, walking approximately forty-nine miles beside his wagon to carry the pails of water and fish. He refreshed the water at each opportunity and scrambled precariously down inside the rim to dump his minnows into the blue lake. They disappeared instantly. For several years he thought his work was a failure. Then a great game rainbow trout was caught in the lake. Careful measurements recorded its length as thirty inches, which is definitely outsize for trout of any variety. Other plantings were made in the lake, and the results are notable. Fly fishing is good from the rocks at the edge of the water, or the fishermen may troll from a boat, with an abundance of giant trout waiting for the hook. As in other national park areas, no fishing license is required. Gear and boats can be rented at the lake.

The lake is approached from the west through Medford, Oregon's pear-growing metropolis. The highway follows the Rogue River, running through forests at the water's edge down below, and climbing through stands of fir, hemlock, and other evergreens to skirt the upper canyons. Coming out on the broad backbone of the Cascades, the highway overlooks the magnificent views eastward and westward, with Klamath Lake shining in the distance, and reveals the white peaks of the Cascades marching away to the north, and Mount Shasta, across the California line (sometimes listed as part of the Cascades, sometimes as part of the Sierras), gleaming white against the sky approximately a hundred miles to the south.

Descending the eastern slope of the range, the highway skirts Diamond Lake, where more hordes of rainbow trout wait hungrily, and runs down through pine forests to a junction with the interstate highway, US-97, which parallels the Cascades on the eastern side.

CHAPTER XVIII

Giant Timber

ALONG IN THE FIFTIES a group of miners panning surface gold high up in the Nevada mountains found their sluice boxes clogged with black, heavy gravel. It was a complaint common to the area; the "black stuff" was a nuisance. Everybody was "pestered" by it. There seemed to be no way to get ride of it.

Then somebody had the black stuff analyzed and found it was more than half silver, with a liberal dash of gold. They dug down and found a body of ore impregnated with the same material. Later surveys revealed that this deposit was several miles long, three hundred or more feet wide, and of unknown depth. It was called the Comstock Lode, the largest concentrated silver deposit in the history of mining.

The viewpoint of the first Comstock miners toward the black gravel was duplicated by the annoyance of the Oregon country pioneers toward the timber that stretched in a practically unbroken stand from the crest of the Cascades to the sea. It was broken only by the rivers and lush meadows and open glades of the Willamette Valley, where the Indians had kept large areas burned off to make hunting easier. Once this open country was settled, which was within the first decade after the influx began, the ground must be cleared. The settler was interested only in farming; the timber was a final obstacle barring access to rich, deep soil. It must be cut off, burned off, disposed of in any way possible.

Pioneers writing to relatives and friends "back East" during those early decades either minimized the timber or pretended that it wasn't there. It was considered to be a drawback, a handicap to continued settlement.

But gradually—not suddenly, as with the Comstock Lode —it began to dawn on the new community that here was a great natural resource. Their own local needs for lumber started the industry in a small way. The size and quality of the timber, and its ease of access, indicated that there might be a future in the business. The smoke from small sawmills, whose machinery had been shipped around the Horn, soon began to rise along the west slopes of the Cascades; and presently, as transportation opened the way to more distant markets, first by sea and later augmented by rail, a new and spectacular era was ushered in.

Undreamed of, in the beginning, were the dimensions and value of the treasure. Actually, as it was later appraised— and is still being appraised—it outranked the Comstock by far. The entire yield of the Comstock, in fact, was of less value than today's normal two-year output of timber products in the states of Oregon and Washington.

And while the Comstock today is an abandoned shell, looted and lifeless except for a few stubborn "last-ditch" operations thousands of feet underground, the growing timber of the Cascades area is a perpetual resource. Under

Ray Atkeson

Sunset behind Mount McLaughlin across Klamath Lake in southern Oregon

Ray Atkeson

THE FOREST PRIMEVAL
Half the nation's remaining timber lies west of the Cascades

proper conservation methods—and these are being applied more vigorously year by year—there will be timber as long as the moist winds blow in from the Pacific, snow falls on the Cascades, and melted snow seeps back through the deep soil and tree roots to the sea.

Comprehension bogs down in the presence of the astronomical figures which must be used to describe timber resources of the Cascades area. What, for example, does a thousand *billion* board feet of lumber suggest to the average person? That was the approximate size of the original timber stand in Oregon and Washington. A worker in a sawmill which cuts a million board feet daily—and there are many in the Northwest—has some faint glimmering of a notion of what the statement means. It means that his "million-a-day" mill would have to work at full capacity each day of the year, except Sundays, for *three thousand years,* to cut that many logs into lumber.

And when the Gargantuan chore was done, and the thirty centuries of labor were over, it would be found that the forest had not been disturbed. There would be a clearing adjacent to the mill, and that is all. Fifteen complete crops of two-hundred-year-old Douglas fir would have come and gone during the interval.

The picture can be imparted only through comparative and relative means. Though great inroads have been made during the last half century, the remaining timber in Oregon and Washington, largely in the watershed of the Cascades, comprises about half the timber resources of the United States and is by far the globe's largest and heaviest per-acre stand. From the summit of Mount Rainier, on a clear day, more than a third of the nation's timber is within view.

How such prodigious quantities of any vegetation can be concentrated even in such a large area is explained by the size of the individual trees. A full-grown Douglas fir is one of the largest of living things, being second in bulk only to the sequoia. The mature tree—which was larger than the average pine when Columbus put forth westward from Spain—is commonly six to eight feet in diameter at the ground and up to three hundred feet in height, or the approximate level of the thirtieth floor of a modern office building. It will have bark a foot thick and no branches mar its stately column for a sheer ninety feet, when limbs thicker than a man's body thrust out, supporting foliage which covers a rough circle perhaps a hundred feet in diameter. The needles are smaller than those of the pine and of a dark green which never varies in hue, winter or summer.

A single Douglas fir will produce more than twenty thousand board feet of lumber, or enough to build four average five-room bungalows. The first ninety feet, up to the limbs, are the "peeler logs," from which plywood and veneers are made, and also produce what is generally agreed to be the finest construction lumber known. Special saws are required to fell the giant, special, heavy-duty equipment to haul it from the woods and reduce it to dimension lumber. Manufacturing plants making this equipment alone are among the largest in the Northwest.

Such a forest monarch is, of course, the "cream of the cream," the result of the most favorable combination of soil, drainage, and wind currents, and towers above its lesser neighbors. Yet an average stand of untouched Douglas fir— what the loggers call a "good show"—will produce sixty-five to seventy thousand board feet per acre, a square mile close to fifty million. Multiply that square mile many times, with vast intervening acres yielding half as much per acre but still profitable for large-scale logging operations; envision the timber as a green blanket covering the 500-mile length of the Cascades, over an average width of a hundred and fifty miles between the Cascades and the sea—broken by farm lands constituting less than 20 per cent of the whole—and a dim perspective of the planet's greatest forest begins to take form.

It would be a pleasure to record that this vast treasure chest was divided equally among the settlers of the Oregon country, and that the business of acquiring title to timber-lands was carried out in an honest orderly fashion by hard-working men. The truth is that the era of expansion was ushered in by some of the most amazing exploitation in the nation's history.

Settlement was encouraged in the beginning by means of land grants of 320 acres to single men and a full square mile to men with families. Under this "donation land claim" system much of the low-lying timbered areas passed quickly into private ownership. In the vast slopes of the Cascades, however, the land was too steep and too remote from settlements to attract those interested solely in farming, and these public lands were sold as "timber claims" at prices ranging from a dollar and a quarter to two-fifty per acre. Since an acre might produce enough lumber to build a substantial village, and could be turned over immediately to specu-lators at a tenfold profit, it soon dawned on the public at large that there was "gold in the hills."

Part of the blame for the era of timber grabbing that swept like wildfire through the length of the Cascades can be placed on the timber laws themselves, which were an invitation to mass looting. A part of the responsibility can be charged to the Administration in Washington, whose remote-control "specialists," as is usually the case, knew nothing of local conditions.

But much of the unholy credit must be given directly to the average citizen himself; to the flaw in human nature—or, more charitably, a species of mob psychology—which causes otherwise respectable citizens to rush in with the crowd and help themselves, once the store windows are smashed. Moreover, the amazing corruption of public officials during this epoch was rooted in the same flaw; as good servants of a public which was itself corrupt, it was all too easy to swim with the tide.

Theoretically timber claims were sold for individual use and benefit, but nothing in the law precluded an individual from acquiring as many claims as he liked. Thus business-men in small towns could, and did, buy up a quarter or half section, hire workmen to build a log cabin and clear an acre or two of land. Having lived in the cabin for a pleasant week or so during the summer, thus complying with the strict letter of the law, the new owners could sell the claims at ten to twenty times their original cost. The next logical step was to file simultaneously on three or four or a dozen adjoining tracts, build cabins on each, move from one to the other with camp outfits during the summer, and "cash in." Then portable "cabins" of flimsy box construction were dragged from claim to claim, and the proper number of witnesses secured at each stopping place as proof of "actual residence."

Soon all pretense was abandoned. Newly formed companies bent on acquiring timberland in large tracts simply rounded up a group of workmen, or sailors on shore leave, paid them five dollars each for both timber application and assignment, and filed sheafs of papers covering ownership of thousands of acres. The final and natural step was to side-step even this formality and forge the signatures. When more than one huge block had been reduced to stumps, the mill dismembered, and the principals scattered to new fields, it was discovered that titles were adorned with a rich army of mythical Smiths, Joneses, and Robinsons.

An amazing glimpse of this buccaneer era is furnished by one Stephen A. Douglas Puter, self-styled "King of the Oregon Land Fraud Ring," who set down some of his experiences in a book entitled *Looters of the Public Domain*.[1] Whether inspired by remorse or exhibitionism—a moot point—Puter's account of the methods used by the plundering army leaves nothing to the imagination.

It appears that Puter served his apprenticeship in Humboldt County, in northern California, when a large tract was thrown open for entry. He knew all the best claims in this tract, and charged twenty-five dollars to point them out, twenty-five dollars to build a cabin of split boards twelve by sixteen feet by seven feet high, including one window, a board floor, and a wooden fireplace. (Puter pauses to note, with morbid amusement, that occasionally a settler built such a "house" from a packing box of twelve by sixteen *inches*, and set it on his timber claim so that he could later swear to legal "improvement.")

The entrymen scarcely slept in Puter's cabins, but ac-

---

[1] Portland Printing House, 1908. A collector's item, one of the few existing copies is included in the files of the Oregon Historical Society.

quired title in eight to ten months, claiming continuous
residence. Puter then acted as agent and negotiated sales
for the claims at eight to twelve hundred dollars for each
160 acres. The buyers resold to a sawmill company at four
thousand dollars per claim. (This was in 1876. By 1908 these
timberlands were valued at two to three hundred dollars
per acre, or thirty to forty thousand dollars for each 160
acres.)

Inspired by a dawning "How long has this been going
on?" enthusiasm, Puter began to work north. At Eureka,
near the Oregon line, he glimpsed a new and rich field of
corruption. A company there was hiring men to file on
timber claims. No personal examination of the tract was required of the entryman; he must merely appear at the land
office, show citizenship or first papers, and entry would be
allowed. The company took care of all other details—the
filing fees and "paper work"—and was rushing men in by
the hundreds. Puter personally saw twenty-five sailors from
"Coffee Jack's" boardinghouse, in Eureka, go to the county
courthouse to get their first papers, then to the land office
to file, then to a notary public to execute a blank deed, then
receive $50 each and return to Coffee Jack's, all in a single
tour. The company then filled in the descriptions of choice
tracts, acquired title the moment the land was thrown open
for entry, and resold to a larger "syndicate."

It was the aftermath of this deal which stirred Puter's
kindling enthusiasm. The syndicate felt that the final $25
patent fee was too large and sent an attorney to Washington
to negotiate for smaller fees. Instead the general land office
suspended all claims and sent an agent out to investigate "al-
leged frauds." Three of these agents were met by the syndi-

cate, entertained, and "influenced" to send back favorable reports. The fourth could not be bought and sent in true reports which resulted in the forfeiture of one hundred and fifty-odd claims. The principals were indicted and brought to trial, but through one legal device after another these trials dragged on through the months and years.

That three of four federal agents could be corrupted opened up new vistas for Puter. He came up into Oregon (1888) and found the forests alive with timbermen. Capitalists from Michigan, Wisconsin, and Minnesota were on the ground, eager to invest and willing to ask no questions. Soon learning his way about, and being an expert timber cruiser, Puter lost no time in locating the choicest tracts. He sold this information to investors, acquired capital, enlarged his acquaintanceship among federal agents and speculators; and presently was the acknowledged leader of the racketeers.

Puter's specialty was not only dealing in timberlands obtained by fraud but his ability to "influence" federal agents who might later prove troublesome. One of his typical deals illustrates the devious technique followed by the "timber wolves" of that ruthless epoch.

Under the Timber and Stone Act—Puter's favorite among the many futile legislative gestures designed to protect the "public interest"—the filing fee on a quarter section of 160 acres was thirty dollars, the cost of the land three dollars and a half per acre, or a total of five hundred and ninety dollars for the claim. Puter was already in league with a United States district attorney with whom he always consulted in setting the stage for a fraudulent deal. He also had on his secret pay roll an agent of the federal land office who was useful in giving him advance information as to when a certain tract would be thrown open for entry, and in incidental ways. Also Puter had capitalists ready to buy the fraudulently acquired timber, and an army of workmen to carry out the actual machinery of the fraud.

Advised by his federal land agent that a new and magnificent area would soon be opened, Puter sent forty men into the area to locate two claims each, or a total of 12,800 acres. He sent in two expert workmen (at a dollar and a half per day) to build a cabin on each tract. He paid a United States deputy surveyor five dollars to insert the forty names in his survey of the tract and attest that each was already in residence—which would give the forty the first chance to file when the tract was opened. Now all was ready for the Government to declare the area open for settlement.

While waiting for this deal to "jell" the industrious Puter, who was no man to permit grass to grow under his feet, went down to Salem (the state capital) to look into the school land situation. He promptly uncovered a bonanza. When school lands were set apart, out of the state's share of the public land, the federal Government agreed to reimburse the state for such school lands by turning over an equal acreage of the public domain.

Puter discovered that these timbered areas could be purchased at a dollar and a quarter per acre, regardless of their obvious value. He accordingly located several thousand acres, sold them to one of his waiting capitalists at two dollars and a half per acre, in cash, then purchased the land from the state at a dollar and a quarter per acre, keeping the balance for himself. Thus, without investing a cent of his own capital, he netted some fifteen thousand dollars while waiting for the "big deal" to develop.

Unfortunately, on this school deal, it had been necessary to take in a partner named Jones; and Jones—so Puter relates with tremendous indignation—was himself no mediocre pirate. Learning from Puter how the "big deal" was set up, Jones worked fast. When the rich federal timberland was finally thrown open, Puter found to his amazement and horror that all the choice tracts located by his forty stooges had been filed on by the state as indemnity school lands. Furthermore, the man who had already bought the school lands—taking a leaf from Puter's own book—was Jones. To add insult to injury, Jones was able to acquire the 12,800 choice acres at a dollar and a quarter per acre—after Puter had obligingly paid all the location costs!

Enraging as this cutthroat gesture was to Puter, his pride suffered a further blow. He had already promised his forty helpers eight hundred and thirty-five dollars each, plus five dollars per tract to his friendly United States surveyor for attesting that the forty were "old settlers"; and to pay this out of his own pocket rather than out of profits on the deal was unthinkable. Moreover, Jones knew too much about Puter's forty settlers—not to mention the relatively puny state land deal—to make a legal issue of it.

So Puter went to the United States attorney who had long been on his pay roll—and received his final lesson in human depravity. With unconscious humor, in astonishment and pain, he relates that his trusted United States attorney had actually been in league with Jones all the while! This meant that Puter, in a manner of speaking, had not only had his throat cut but had been entirely decapitated. The attorney and Jones did quite well on the deal. The land had cost them two hundred and five dollars per quarter section and was later sold for forty-eight hundred dollars per quarter section. Puter blackmailed both and got mediocre amounts from them, a puny take compared to the fortune that had been almost within his grasp.

At the close of his spectacular career, as Puter admits philosophically, he was penniless. Mild retribution finally overhauled him: he was forced to spend seventeen months in the Multnomah County (Portland) jail. Even then, as he points out with melancholy pride, when the buccaneer era had drawn to a close—the stable door locked after the incalculably valuable horse was stolen—Puter still had sufficient influence to secure a presidential pardon and thus evade serving the final five months of his two-year sentence.

Altogether two thirds or more of the magnificent timber stands in this area passed into private hands before the federal Government and the state legislatures could collect themselves to halt the organized looting. Then the clock could not be turned backward. There is today no restraint on the cutting of timber on privately owned stands. The states and the forest service can only guard what they have, and move toward picking up sections and areas of cutover land, denuded of its timber but capable of producing new crops for future generations. As land like this is thrown back on the county for non-payment of taxes, it is gradually acquired for state reserves, and will again someday produce its full quota of timber, unless erosion has washed away much of its soil.

It is estimated that the private stands of timber will be exhausted in a matter of twenty years, except where some company has secured enough land in its own right to continue operations indefinitely. Some of the larger companies, looking ahead, are setting up a "sustained yield" system that will assure them of a supply of timber for perhaps centuries to come. Nevertheless the nation faces a timber shortage in the not so distant future, when timber and wood products will rise in price and the supply diminish to an inconvenient level. This period of shortage will be alleviated by the national forest reserves now guarded and protected, and by state forests still uncut.

Under the sustained yield program the manager of a forest figures the time necessary for a tree to grow in his area from seed to marketable size. He then surveys carefully the trees available and marks the ones for cutting, advising his crews how to fell the timber without damaging new growth. Under this system the debris must be cut and piled for burning whenever it is safe to burn, so that the fire hazard will be reduced to the minimum. Along with this precaution goes the plan of reseeding bare areas where seed trees are not standing sufficiently close to reseed naturally.

Federal forest reserves along the Cascades include close to twenty million acres, much of it the finest kind of timber. The entire length of the Cascade Range is included in one or another of the national forests, lying border to border, each about a million acres in extent. Far down on the western slope of the range the national forests include the gigantic stands of Douglas fir, mixed with Western hemlock (chiefly used here for pulp and paper making), and the Western red cedar (which furnishes shingles for the nation), and adjoining the national forests are state-owned forests reaching farther down toward the valley. On the dry eastern side of the Cascades these forest reserves include millions of acres of Western white pine, a valuable construction wood and increasingly used for interior finish.

The growing cycle for the moist western slope is thirty to fifty years to bring a tree to marketable size, and there is no reason why the forests should not continue to yield, from public-owned reserves alone, close to the minimum required by the nation. The growing cycle on the eastern slopes is, however, between a hundred and two hundred years, since the trees depend for moisture chiefly on the spring melting of snow and must spend the rest of the year enduring drought and cold. In addition to the areas in public ownership, there are about a million acres included in Indian lands and administered by the Indian Service under a system comparable to the management of the forest service.

The national forests were set aside originally as much for their recreation values as for timber, since President Theodore Roosevelt, a great lover of the outdoors, was impressed fully as much by the need for preserving vacation grounds as timber. With this theory no fault is to be found, since the result will be to reserve the entire crest of the Cascades and its sentinel peaks for the use and enjoyment of the public forever.

CHAPTER XIX

Cascades Indians

THE COAST INDIANS of the Cascades area were not warlike. Their country supported them in comparative luxury, and if they ever went hungry it was due to their own neglect in not storing sufficient food. Summer and winter the climate was moderate, and the tribes could keep warm with the minimum of clothing or none at all. They need not search for food, with berries, wild fruits, the hazelnut, and the acorn easily gathered and stored for winter. The wapatoo, a mealy bulb of the swamps, alone was enough to support life. The smaller game animals and the native game birds scattered in droves out of every clump of underbrush. Wild ducks covered the surface of the swamps. The smelt, a tiny fat fish, running into their favorite streams early in March, crowded them literally from bank to bank, and could be taken in willow scoops, strung up to dry from the roof beams of the lodge, and there wait for winter needs as food, or would even serve as a candle to light the winter night. Salmon came crowding into the coast rivers in May and again in the autumn, in such numbers that no man needed anything more than a forked stick to fetch out his year's supply. The ocean shore, too, offered shellfish, schools of herring, sleeping seals that could be speared from the rocks, and occasionally a dead whale washed up on the sands to provide a feast for all.

With no need to go beyond their immediate neighborhood for food, the coast Indians could lose themselves a matter of thirty miles from home. The tribes grew fat, squat, slow of movement, and mild of disposition. The need for battle was not urgent, unless a neighbor offered insult, or a northern tribe from the Puget Sound area or southern Alaska came by canoe to capture a few able-bodied ones for slaves. Occasionally a party of inland warriors crossed the Cascades, bent on raiding, but these must run the gantlet of the predatory Columbia gorge warriors.

The coast Indians knew a variety of foods, most of them cooked, and each could be stored for winter by the women. They did not cultivate the Indian corn nor any garden, not even tobacco, since they could smoke the fragrant leaves of the kinnikinnick, a low-growing shrub along the coast. Their life permitted them a fixed habitation, and they set up huge lodges of cedar trunks forty to sixty feet long, with room inside for four to a dozen families. They boiled their food in baskets or in vessels carved from wood, into which they placed water and hot stones. They also roasted and baked in pits covered with moss and earth, and broiled meat on spits.

Fasting, steam baths, and a noisy intervention by the medicine men sufficed to cure most ills, and if the patient died he was laid out with elaborate ceremony in a richly decorated canoe, loaded with his immediate possessions, ready for his spirit trip to the "Land Beyond the Ocean."

This disposal of a man's possessions left his heirs without accumulated wealth and kept the tribes in a state of communal poverty.

Their life of leisure and comparative peace gave them time for storytelling and the weaving of legends. And in this Cascades coastal area there developed the Indian "universal language," the Chinook jargon, common to no tribe but known to all the tribes from California to Alaska and east to the Rocky Mountains.

When the white man came to the region he found the coast Indians mild-tempered and lazy with good living. Within a generation the tribes were hangers-on of the white settlements, abandoning their own habits and customs, in which they seemed to take little pride, to ape the new race. The earliest Indian reservations set up by the United States were in the Cascades area, and were primarily to protect the peaceful tribes from the inland warriors, and incidentally to relieve the white settlers of the hordes of begging, pilfering Indians who hung about the cabin doors.

A different picture was presented by the tribes living on the high plateau east of the Cascades. While scarcely a hundred miles from the "Land of Plenty" and separated from it only by the mountain barrier, they were different in temper, physique, and habit.

The high plateau was mostly a barren and hungry land. The tribes must fight to protect any natural bulb garden that would furnish food, since the neighboring tribe was equally hungry. Good hunting areas were contested bitterly. Each season of the year meant a journey to a new place in search of food, and probably a battle when they arrived. Winter was a time for withdrawing into holes or half-buried tepees to live out the bitter winter. In early times they must have done their marching on foot, dragging their light tepee poles and skin shelters behind them. Then the horse returned to his ancient home, probably in the eighteenth century, and was seized on by the plains Indians as perhaps the greatest boon in their entire history. Now the tribes could extend their range, fight more effectively, and speed their march from food place to food place.

So the white man found the Indian, fierce, proud, daring in battle, eager to make war, and eternally hungry. It was the inland Indian who harassed the white settlers and forced development of the west of the Cascades, where there was no Indian trouble.

Both types of Indians are living on reservations in the Cascades area today, and the contrast between them is still marked.

The Indian of the present day lives mainly on whatever is left of the reservation lands allotted to his forefathers from about 1855 to 1875, and administered under varying theories formulated by Congress and the Office of Indian Affairs, which is part of the Department of the Interior.

Reservations were held intact at first, except as white settlers invaded them in search of gold or timber, until 1887, when the Indian Allotment Act provided that Indian lands must be divided into homesteads and shared among the Indians, each of whom would receive title to his homestead when he proved himself competent to handle his own affairs. Until he received title to his allotment he remained a ward of the Government, with his land and money held in trust. With the land title, once he had achieved it, came full citizenship and a new status as a "competent" Indian, which cut him off from the guardianship of the Office of Indian Affairs and put him legally on a par with the white citizens.

Along with this effort to Americanize the first Americans went the policy of breaking up the tribes, educating the children in schools off the reservation, discouraging and sometimes forbidding the tribal dances and other ceremonies, and attempting to substitute ordinary American gear for the old-time costumes, ornaments, and utensils.

In cases where the tribal lands were more than sufficient to cover the allotments to members of the tribe the surplus land was to be sold off, opened to white settlement or otherwise disposed of, to break up the reservation. In the Siletz Reservation, for instance, west of the Cascades, one and a third million acres of some of the finest timberland in the region was given by treaty to remnants of a dozen different tribes. When the time came to allot homesteads only about three hundred family heads were on hand, and less than fifty thousand acres were needed to satisfy the allotment law. The vast acreages of timber remaining were regarded as "surplus" and passed, by lawful or unlawful means, into white hands.

The allotment plan continued until 1932, when the "New Deal for the Indians" was instituted. By that time much of the best land was gone, some reservations were broken up entirely, and half the Indian population had been declared "competent" and were no longer wards of the Government. Disease and hunger were again taking their ancient toll, and the Indian was regarded as a dying race.

"Competent" Indians were permitted to live where they pleased, and on them were laid the burdens of taxpaying, earning their own living, educating their own children, and all the multiple problems of ordinary life, along with a privilege or two not possessed by their "ward" brothers, such as buying liquor as freely as they wished, attending public schools without paying tuition, and appealing to the ordinary courts of justice for protection.

The "ward," on the other hand, was still watched over by the Indian Service, his money handled in trust, his legal affairs carried on in federal courts, and his ancient rights of fishing, hunting, and behaving as he wished on the reservation defended for him by the Indian Service officials.

Since the difference between a competent Indian and a ward Indian depends on whether or not his father or grandfather secured title to the land allotment, or whether he himself decided to crawl out from the benevolent wing of the Indian Service, the picture is a little complicated. An Indian may be full-blooded or of mixed parentage, he may resemble an Indian or a white, but his legal status can be determined only by an exhaustive research into the history of his family with relation to the tribal lands. In some instances even the Indian Service is unable to decide precisely whether the individual can be classed as Indian ward or Indian competent. Since the abundant funds of the Indian Service must be spent on the ward Indians, while the others help pay the bills through taxation, the "Indian question" has many ramifications.

Meanwhile a health program among the Indians has changed him from a dying race to a race with the largest birth rate of any racial group in the United States, and whatever problems are inherent in him are by way of being doubled and trebled as his numbers increase.

The Indian New Deal goes back in a fashion to the pre-allotment period. Once again the tribes are being organized, even though a "tribe" may consist of remnants of twenty-five or more tribes, perhaps some of them hereditary enemies, and their offspring mixed with white, Negro, Oriental, or Filipino blood. What is left of the tribal lands are withdrawn from entry, and an effort is under way to help the Indian return to the old community life that is presumably natural to him. The competent men, of course, have passed from the jurisdiction of the Indian Service, except in cases where the individual retained his tribal affiliations, so the newly organized Indian communities represent perhaps one half of the Indian population. Nevertheless the old flavor is returning to the Indian reservations.

Once again the tribal council sits in the community house, and the Indian schools are set up on the reservation to teach the children to live in their own environment. The old dances are being relearned, and even though the tutors may be public welfare workers instead of the old ones of the tribe, the effects are colorful. With this return to the old ways goes an entirely modern program of sanitation, public health, medical and dental care, and a vigorous attempt to lead the tribes into some community, agricultural, stock-raising, or commercial activity that will bring self-support.

Since each reservation is handled as a unit, with no exchange of tribal funds, each Indian community lives as its financial affairs permit. Some reservation lands are rich and productive, some barren. These differences exist in the reservations now operating in the Cascades area.

The coast Indians around the lower Columbia River have been exposed to association with the whites for more than a century—more perhaps than any other group in the United States—and are, perhaps as a consequence, among the least romantic of the natives. Three large reservation areas are maintained along the coast, and here are found the descendants of the tribes that once crowded this lush area.

South of the Columbia River, near the Siletz and Rogue rivers, are found a thousand or so of the coast Indians, in the reservations known as Grand Ronde, Siletz, and the Rogue River communities. A few women make baskets of hazel withes, spruce root, maidenhair fern, et cetera, for sale. Sometimes dolls are displayed with the traditional dress of peace, war, or ceremonial. Wild blackberry jam is canned for commercial trade. Otherwise the community is typically American. The tribes hold an annual festivity in the form of a barbecue and clam feed which echoes something of the ancient salmon ceremonial feast. The coast Indians are at a disadvantage in dressing in the costumes of their ancestors, since this mild climate permitted the tribes to go entirely naked most of the year.

North of the Columbia River, in the remoteness of the Olympic Peninsula, three thousand or so Indians live on several reservations more remote from populated centers. These have kept more of the ways of their fathers, and their hand-carved canoes and baskets are authentic Indian artistry. Their skill in water sports, either on lakes, rivers, or the tumbling surf of the ocean shore, is unmarred by white influence.

The Quinault Reservation alone includes 111,000 acres of heavily timbered hills skirting the sea, with giant firs, spruce, and cedar and some of the best fishing and hunting in the

Pacific Northwest. Included in the reservation is beautiful Lake Quinault and the entire length of the Quinault River. The lake is rimmed with great forests and well populated with trout. Indians rent boats and fishing gear to guests at the well-appointed inn. Indian guides seek out the elk and bear for hunters, or guide fishermen to remote trout streams in the virgin forest. Any visitor who craves excitement can engage to be taken down the Quinault River, through white water and tumbling rapids, and out into the ocean, through the surf, in a breath-taking half day of adventure.

At the tip of the Olympic Peninsula is a small reservation for the Makah tribe, remnants of the Indians who once gained their main living from the sea. This tribe has kept its right to fish for fur seals and sea otter, with its ancient claims protected, even though the United States, Great Britain, Russia, and Japan agreed to permit the fur seals to pass unmolested to their breeding grounds in the Pribilof Islands. Through the international negotiations the United States scrupulously protected the rights of the Makah tribe, and the visitor can be treated to an occasional sight of the capture of a fur seal.

Near the Canadian border several small reservations are strung along the narrow coast strip, where the Cascades approach the ocean. Indians and "breeds" of the Swinomish, Puyallup, Muckleshoot, Tulalip, and other reservations live by fishing, clam digging, and hunting, with a bit of agriculture. These tribes show something of the influence of northern tribes in using the totem pole, a symbol virtually unknown to the other natives of the Cascades area.

This group of tribes has a typical old-time celebration, held annually to commemorate Treaty Day. Near-by tribes gather in the Swinomish "long house"—a traditional community dwelling—and keep the fires burning night and day with feasting and dancing. Solo dancers rattle their shell and bone ornaments until they work themselves to a frenzy, squaws do a slow dance to a certain ancient chant, and old tongues are loosened again to tell tales of the old days.

East of the Cascades the descendants of the warlike inland tribes are gathered into three reservations on the slopes of the Cascades and two others set across the high plateau at a safe distance from their hereditary enemies. These reservations, of course, were set up many years ago, and the blood-curdling yell of the Umatillas hasn't stiffened the hair on the Klamath spine for many a year, but nevertheless it is well to maintain the distance.

The Yakima Reservation has a population of about three thousand, mostly on small allotments. A good deal of tribal lands remains in the reservation and forms a nucleus for a co-operative venture in cattle raising. The group here borrowed about fifteen hundred head of cattle from the federal Government (to be repaid in kind) and are conducting a business that has netted them close to two hundred and seventy-five thousand dollars in the last six years and promises even greater profits. The cattlemen follow the usual range practice of wintering the stock on home farms or the open range, and driving them in summer to the lush new grass on the high Cascades. When the cattle buyers come the Indians, in "ten-gallon" hats and boots, mounted on cow ponies, bring in the wild cattle, haze them into corrals, and cut them out, one at a time, to be driven into the sales arena, where the buyers perch on the fence making their bids.

These Indian families harvest hops, pick huckleberries

from the Cascades slope for drying and canning, weave baskets, and create a fascinating array of buckskin clothing for sale. These inland tribes traditionally wore beaded and fringed garments, with feathered headdresses for gala occasions. Their beaded and quilled moccasins are their pride and are an attraction for visitors, and their skill with horses is displayed on any excuse. Between ceremonials the younger ones dress in whatever is modern at the moment, while the older members lean toward the bright red or green shirt, gay bandannas, shawls, and the old-time moccasins.

The Warm Springs Reservation, south of the Columbia, has about three hundred thousand acres of land on the eastern slope of the Cascades, most of it barren range land and sparse timber. The best farming spots were allotted long ago, and tribal lands are not sufficient to maintain the population of seven to eight hundred Indians. They have been helped by Government handouts for years, and only recently have they come close to supporting themselves. Never unfriendly to the whites, these Indians helped against the fierce Modocs in the Indian wars of 1872, and have become more accustomed to depending on the whites than some of their brethren. Now their grazing land is being built up again for cattle, and timber sales will bring a few dollars yearly for each member of the tribe. Their ancient fishing rights in the Columbia River are assured to them in perpetuity, and each year the tribe swarms around Celilo Falls, at the eastern end of the Columbia gorge, to spear and net the salmon as it leaps through the white water.

The Klamath tribe—population about 1500; tribes represented, 35—near the southern end of the high plateau, has more than a million acres of excellent pine timber running up almost to the crest of the Cascades, and lower down has possession of rich grazing lands. Some farming, a bit of seasonal work in the potato fields, huge bands of cattle, and a cozy income from timber sales makes the Klamath tribesman a life to be envied by every other Indian in the area. In 1928 the timber cut from the Klamath Reservation, and paid for in cash to the tribe, was sufficient to build a sidewalk eight feet wide from the summit of the Cascades to Washington, D.C.

Across the width of the plateau from the Cascades, near Pendleton, is the Umatilla Reservation, with about twelve hundred descendants of the Cayuse, Umatilla, and Walla Walla tribes, whose ancestors lifted the scalps of many a white in the days of the Oregon Trail. They make a living now from wheat growing, cattle raising, and incidental work, including an annual parade in full war paint at the Pendleton Roundup. Their tepees, set up in traditional style, can occasionally be seen from the highway, as they pause here or there as the mood strikes. With an independence characteristic of their tribes, these Indians carry on their ceremonials without benefit of tourist audiences. In fact, when they forbid white attendance, it is wise indeed to heed the warning.

The Colville and Spokane reservations, in the northeastern corner of the state of Washington, were generously endowed when first set aside, but the discovery of gold in the timbered hills around 1890 cut down some of the Indian privacy, and the Grand Coulee Dam, a colossal setup on the Columbia River, has drowned their traditional fishing grounds at Kettle Falls on the upper Columbia. These

Indians live precariously on the proceeds of intermittent farming, berrying, incidental work, and the sale of timber from their tribal lands.

The Indian religion of the Cascades area was closely connected with everyday life and directed rather toward maintaining their food supply than their morals. For instance, the Spirit of the Salmon was immortal, with the salmon itself regarded somewhat as the fruit of a tree which could be used without detriment or loss to the Spirit, but must be gathered with apologies, thanks, and due dignity. Other ceremonials, religious taboos, dances, and the rules for the behavior of women were tied in with the food gathering or success in battle. When the old ways were abandoned and food came to them without any apparent regard for the Spirit of the Salmon or any other spirit, much of the Indian religion was forgotten. Denominational missionaries vied with each other to win the undoubtedly religious spirit of the Indian, and the incidental friction between the denominations caused the untutored native not a little mystification. Finally the Indians developed a church of their own, which is believed to be a native growth of the Cascades area. This church is called the Indian Shaker Church and has no affiliations with any other Shaker denomination, or indeed with any one denomination of any sort.

Its origin is told as follows. In the late years of the last century one Mudbay Charlie lived and rioted among the coast tribes north of the Columbia River. He was a *cultus* Indian. This adjective, part of the old Chinook jargon, indicates that he was of low moral type and much given to drunkenness, stealing, and infidelity, along with being totally unreliable in money matters. When he died his worn-out body was prepared for burial, for, whatever his faults, Mudbay Charlie was a member of the tribe and must be placed in his decorated canoe, with food and weapons to support his spirit on its journey to the "Land Beyond the Ocean," where his ancestors waited, possibly with some dismay.

But while the attendants were gone to secure the burial trappings the spirit of Mudbay Charlie winged its way upward to the gates of the New Jerusalem and met the disapproving gaze of St. Peter. "You are not fit to die," said the saint sternly. "You must go back and start a church, and teach your brethren that they must not lie nor steal nor become drunken. Tell them to go to church every Sunday. Build churches for them. Go now and earn your right to enter here."

When the attendants returned to the body of Mudbay Charlie they found the spirit back in the body, but it was a different spirit now. Up he rose and organized the Indian Shaker Church. Its creeds are obscure, but its ceremonials are such as to startle the imagination, being a composite of any detail the Indians liked about any denomination they had encountered, including the mummery of the old-time medicine men.

Chants may be High Church with an Indian cadence; processionals verge on the Indian dance. Out of the blackness of a session, lighted only by flickering candles, comes the ringing of bells and the rattle of an old bone "spirit chaser" created before Mount Hood assumed its blanket of eternal snow. Sickness can be treated by drawing the evil from the body with hooked fingers that gather up the invisible evil and fling it into a burning flame. The Indian Shaker Church has a wide following among the tribes on both sides of the Cascades. Adherents are sincere in their attitude toward the ceremonies. Visitors are not welcomed, and the mysteries of the church are performed for the Indian alone.

CHAPTER XX

Old Song and Story

THE INDIAN MIND turned naturally to the snow mountains that dominate the sky line. Many of their legends concern these peaks. They cannot be compared with the Greek myths and scriptural stories in imagery and language. Centuries of handling and rehandling in written form, with interpretation by poetic minds through the ages, have polished the older stories and given them depth and meaning that possibly were not present in the original forms.

Indian myths are told in halting speech, translated from one language to another whose idioms do not coincide. Gestures must take the place of words when the right word cannot be found. Their immediate form depends on the withered lips of the Old Ones, and these ancients of the tribe may have good memories without necessarily a poetic imagination. However, the raw material is here, and in centuries to come the Indian legends may be changed to poetry fit to rank with the old myths more familiar to us.

The stories that follow are not literal reports of any specific interview, but approximations of legends told and re-told in many forms.

WHY THERE ARE NO SNAKES ON MOUNT RAINIER

The Indian word for snow peak was *tacoma* or *Tahoma*, and this was their name for the highest snow peak of the Cascades (now called Mount Rainier), as one would say "The Mountain." Indian tradition made The Mountain a sanctuary where one who fled could no longer be pursued, and criminals and cowards could go into the presence of the Great Spirit to do penance. No Indian could be persuaded to ascend beyond the mountain meadows. He would not bring disaster on himself by setting foot on the eternal snows above the timber line. This was because The Mountain was a high place and not to be profaned.

A long, long time ago the Great Spirit looked down from The Mountain on his people and found them evil, and there were evil ones among the animals too. He decided to blot them out in one great flood, but first he must make a way of escape for the good animals and one good man. He ordered the good man to shoot his arrow into a cloud that hung heavy over The Mountain.

The arrow stuck fast in the cloud, and into its shaft the next arrow penetrated and held, and presently, after much shooting of arrows, there hung a chain of arrows from the cloud down to the valley. Up this chain the good man sent his wife and children, and after them the good animals, inching their way to safety, while below them the waters of the flood rose. When all were safe he hastened to follow. When he reached the cloud he looked back and saw the bad animals and snakes climbing the chain to escape the flood.

He broke the chain of arrows, and they fell backward into the waters that rose even to the snow line of The

Mountain. When presently the flood went away, and the chosen ones could descend, they found no more bad animals or snakes on the slopes of The Mountain, and since that day there have been none.

How Coyote Stole the Fire

The lesser spirits who dwelt high on The Mountain warmed themselves with fire, but the mortals below shivered in the winter cold. The Coyote took counsel with himself and decided to dare the wrath of Those by treading on the sacred snows, that he might bring fire down to the lodges of his friends.

He did not know that the other animals followed him to spy out his bold project. Up the snowy slopes he stole, and while the Watchers drank and feasted he snatched up a coal and fled down the snow.

Instantly the Eternal Ones were in pursuit, and the avalanche, the windstorm, and the ice showered down after him. Before his feet opened up the dread fissures in the ice where Death lives. Coyote sank exhausted at the edge of timber line, unable to go on. From his hiding place behind a tree Fox leaped out, snatched the burning coal, and flashed away through the open forest aisles, with vengeance thundering at his tail. So the Fox, too, made his run, but when the open aisles gave way to the thick underbrush Fox was tangled there, and the Eternal Ones were upon him. So overhead came Squirrel, to whisk up the prize and leap from bough to bough like the flick of a shadow. The Pursuers were weary now, but they spread out craftily, knowing the lower edge of the forest was at hand and Squirrel could not keep up his race across the open plain. But there at the edge of the plain Antelope waited, swifter than the wind, and above him hovered Eagle, and the Dove, and in its turn the tiny Hummingbird, swifter than the glance of the eye. So the Pursuers gave up the chase, and fire was brought to the lodges of the tribes.

LEGEND OF MOUNT MAZAMA

The dark spirit who ruled the Beneath Land was named Llao. He lived in the high mountain above the Klamath tribe. He took the shape of a man and visited the tribe, where he saw and craved the daughter of the chief, the Maiden whose name cannot be named because she is now gone to the land of Death. The Maiden was swift and graceful as a deer, and fair as dawn, and her voice was like the sound of whispering waters.

Llao demanded the Maiden, threatening the tribe. She wept, but told her father she would not bring brave men to death for her sake, so she would give herself up to the dark Llao. But the Maiden was the heart of every man in the tribe, and they said if they must die they would meet their fate like men but would not give up the Maiden.

So Llao thundered from his high mountain, but it was the season of harvest, and even the Dark Spirit was not permitted to begin a war.

In the interval of peace the chief sought the advice of the kindly and smiling Skell, who ruled the sunshine and light and all good things. Skell was wise and gentle, but he, too, had seen the Maiden, and he said, "Give her to me. She shall dwell in the sunshine and braid her hair at the side of the springs. The flowers will bow at her feet. I will defend her against Llao."

So the Maiden wept again, for she wanted nothing but to be a mortal and live like a mortal until death overtook her. Now war between Llao and Skell was inevitable, whatever decision the chief made. Indeed, Llao did not wait for a decision, but opened the war with thunder and threatenings, and a robe of thick smoke about the mountain to hide his plans. Lightning flamed above the smoke, the ground shook, and fire rocks were flung into the air as Llao made the battle and Skell moved to defend the tribe. The smoke covered the land and it was night all over except on the flaming mountain of Llao. The tribesmen hid themselves in caves, afraid to watch the battle. It was during this time that the mountain went down, and the cavern inside the mountain was filled with water, far down inside the rim.

Skell won the battle at long last, and sunshine came again to the land of the Klamaths, only the mountain of Llao was not as before, and the blue lake inside the mountain was not lightly to be looked upon. So the place became a high place for the tribe, not to be spoken of before women. And Skell in his kindness left the Maiden at peace in her lodge.

BRIDGE OF THE GODS

Site of the legendary Bridge of the Gods is in the lower reaches of the Columbia gorge, where the river broke through the backbone of the range. Indian legends in all tribes adjacent to the area insist that a great natural bridge once spanned the river here and that it crashed in comparatively modern times, perhaps within the century before the white men came. Opinion of geologists is divided, one school admitting that the former existence of such a natural wonder is possible, even probable; the other school stating flatly that such a stupendous arch was impossible. The lay observer prefers to believe there was such a bridge. The outward clues suggest it: the great abutments on either side, scoured clean by some comparatively recent landslide, the identical texture of rock on each side, fold by fold; the still debris-choked river below, where, up to two decades ago, full-grown trees could be seen standing upright in the clear depths. As seen from the air, the appearance of a broken arch is most striking.

Now that fire was a possession of the tribes, it was discovered to be a fitful servant, prone to die into blackness when the women turned their backs or the brave set off to pursue a maiden or spear a fish. And of course the fire could be rebuilt only from the fire in some other lodge, and in times of sleep the fires of the whole tribe might be lost. There must, then, be a dependable source—an ever-burning flame—where fire could be had by all.

Pondering this problem, the Great Chief (sometimes a man and sometimes a god, according to the needs of the legend) chose a spot for the ever-burning fire, and a squaw to tend it.

The spot was the center of the bridge that arched the great river. It was a bridge of earth and great rocks, upon which trees grew. Beneath the bridge there was a great falls in the river, which blocked the canoes of the coast tribes from passing the mountains, and also blocked the salmon from the upriver tribes, so they must come to the bridge to trade. They brought buffalo robes, obsidian for arrowheads and their wondrous paint colors, to barter with the coast tribes for the fat salmon.

Yes, the place was chosen well, for all could reach it, north, south, east, and west, and borrow the fire at need. But was the squaw chosen so well? Her name was Loowit, and it was a beautiful name, but Loowit was not beautiful. No, she was old and ugly beyond bearing, and she grew more wrinkled and dry as the years passed, until it was only with averted eyes that the tribesmen could approach her to borrow fire.

But she was faithful and the fire never failed, and the Great Chief, looking down at her work, smiled and bestowed upon her the gift of eternal life. He had given this gift to few others. Immortal was his elder son Klickitat, fierce and hot-blooded in both love and hate. Klickitat dwelt in the land to the north of the great river and ruled the fiercest of the plains Indians. And immortal likewise was the Great Chief's younger son Wyeast, who lived to the south of the river and held the land from the mountains to the sea. Wyeast was young and proud in his strength, slow to anger but mighty of will.

So the Great Chief made Loowit immortal, and she wept.

Moved by her tears, the Great Chief said, "Weep not, Loowit. I thought to please you with this gift. What then would you desire?"

He could not take away eternal life, but any other gift could be added. And so he promised.

Loowit explained her tears. She was old and ugly, and men averted their faces when they came to borrow fire. Now mortal life can be borne with courage, even by the ugly, for who will falter on the hardest march when they know it lasts but a day? Now she must live forever, and there was no release. She could endure only if she were young and beautiful. Tyhee, the Great Spirit, had promised.

He made her young, and beautiful beyond compare, but

his heart misgave him. The new beauty of Loowit astounded all who came to borrow fire. Her fame spread. The gentle and young Wyeast came from the land of the Multnomahs to gaze on the beautiful maiden. He arrived at the Bridge of the Gods just as Klickitat came thundering down from the north on the same errand.

Now the reason the two brothers were widely separated was because of their tempers, which took fire from each other. In fact, long ago Tyhee had separated these two men by the width of the mighty river and the barrier of the mountains, and forbidden each to cross these barriers, or to cross the Bridge of the Gods.

They did not cross. There was no need. Each was at the center of the bridge, and there they fought, and the tribes gathered on either bank to watch the battle. Each was invincible. Were they not immortal? Loowit fled to the green meadow toward the sea and paused in fright and fascination to watch the outcome.

There was no victory possible, as immortal strove against immortal. The damage was all to the battleground itself. Rocks quaked and spouted fire, the mighty bridge came tumbling down, and the great river was dammed high up along the walls of the gorge. It spread into the inland country, so squaws and children fled screaming from the flood. Below the dam the tribes moved hastily and in awe from the banks of the empty river, fearing that the bursting of the dam would sweep all before it.

In pity Tyhee had to end the battle. He came rushing on a mighty wind and gripped a son in either hand.

"Here are two men and but one maiden," said his sons. "We will never cease to fight."

Tyhee had but one course. He turned his gaze on Loowit, standing at the edge of the range, and she changed into a mountain. Because she was beautiful the mountain is a perfect symmetrical cone, rising unbroken from the ever-green timber around it, and dazzling white from timber line to summit. And even as a mountain, Loowit's faithful heart is unchanged. She carries a bit of the eternal fire in her bosom, which breaks out in smoke wreaths when her sorrow comes upon her heavier than she can bear.

Tyhee set Wyeast back upon his tribal lands, and the mountain Wyeast lifts its head arrogantly in its youthful pride. But Klickitat, for all his rough ways, had a tender heart, and he wept to see the beautiful maiden Loowit wrapped in snow. So the mountain Klickitat bends its head forever in sorrow as it gazes down on Loowit in her beauty.

This legend is told in many forms, but always the three Guardian Peaks are etched against the sky to give it authority. The Indian name for the peaks has been changed to Mount St. Helens for the beautiful Loowit, Mount Hood for Wyeast, and Mount Adams for Klickitat. They stand today as Tyhee placed them, a little separated by distance, but grouped together by a great tragedy. And between the warring brothers flows the Columbia River, but the Bridge of the Gods lies forever lost beneath the waters. And when the dam broke the space below the falls was filled, so the river flows down in rapids, up which the salmon can make their way to the farthest inland waters of the river. The salmon are no longer a property of the coast tribes, and the old days of the rich trading are gone forever.

CHAPTER XXI

Fisherman's Valhalla

IRVING COBB once wrote: "Somewhere on this continent there may be better trout fishing than in Central Oregon, but I, personally, have not found it." He was referring to the lakes and streams on the eastern slopes of the Cascades, in the southern section of the range, where a hundred-mile "Century Drive" encircles the headwaters of the Deschutes River and a dozen or more mountain lakes.

In the chill waters of these mountain lakes, in Diamond Lake, farther down the backbone of the range, and in the turbulent Deschutes River are found the largest rainbow trout on record. On exhibition in the offices of the Oregon Fish and Game Commission are the two largest rainbows ever caught. They were taken at Diamond Lake. Each exceeds thirty-six inches in length, and each tipped the scales at slightly more than thirty-five *pounds*.

An article describing these Diamond Lake trout appeared in a national magazine in the early twenties, entitled "Measuring Trout by the Yard," and brought a storm of protest from nimrods throughout the nation. The gist of their criticism was that, while they enjoyed "fish stories" and occasionally indulged in similar flights of fancy themselves, it was unfortunate that a reputable magazine would advance such a fable seriously. Even the photographs of the stream-lined behemoths, with accompanying solemn statements from the Game Commission, failed to silence their raucous outcries.

Only the few doubters who made it a point of personal privilege to fish in Diamond Lake, and personally landed one of the giants, were finally convinced. And it is recorded that some of these, contemplating with astonishment the creature that had been cruising in the frigid depths a few crowded minutes before, reaffirmed the ancient, ultimate expression of awe: "There ain't any sech animal!"

All anglers in Diamond Lake do not drag out trout approaching the maximum in size, but packages of speckled dynamite tipping the scales at eight to ten pounds are not uncommon. They are true rainbow trout, and the sagacious Game Commission takes eggs from this lake to plant in other less favored waters. Rainbows taken from the roaring Deschutes—which falls three thousand feet in a hundred miles and is accordingly lined with riffles and foam-flecked pools which haunt fishermen's dreams during the workaday week—commonly run from two to eight pounds. Huge Dolly Varden trout, sullen and savage fighters, lurk at the bottom of these pools. The largest caught each season—an unofficial competition among inveterate prowlers of the Deschutes—is usually in the neighborhood of fifteen pounds.

To nimrods of this area no other section of the Cascades exists. Yet directly across the Mackenzie Pass, within an hour's drive of the Deschutes, there are Mackenzie River addicts who have never wet a fly east of the range. A little farther south, still on the west side of the barrier, the roots of the Umpqua River spring from the melted snow adjacent to Diamond Lake. Umpqua enthusiasts scorn the Mackenzie, have never seen Diamond Lake, and look down their noses at the famous Rogue, southernmost of the scores of rivers flowing westward from the Cascades.

The Rogue, in turn, is presumed by its admirers to be the principal home of the king of all white-water fighters, the steelhead. Many globe-trotting fishermen who have fished the seven seas, such as the late Zane Grey, have established permanent lodges along the Rogue and assert that this planet offers no greater thrill than to land a twelve-pound steelhead with light tackle.

Up on the Washougal River, a snow-fed stream which rises at the base of Mount Adams and extends a brief but gorgeous thirty miles to join the Columbia just below the gorge, it is fighting talk to suggest that the Rogue is even comparable to the Washougal in the matter of steelhead fishing. And the prowlers of the Trask and Nestucca—to mention only two of the scores of coastal streams—assert that only the bruised and beaten remnants of the steelhead hordes are found in upland waters; the true fighting warriors are close to the sea.

Actually this strange fish is an equally savage battler at tidewater as at two hundred miles inland, since it is as much at home in the river as the sea. It is a true trout, an offshoot of the great rainbow family, which has acquired seagoing habits, coming back to its home river each year to spawn and returning again to the sea. Each round trip finds it bigger and more truculent. At maturity he tips the scales at eight to eighteen pounds—one of the latter, fairly hooked, comprising the final purple passage in the steelhead fancier's career.

Washougal sportsmen carry the business of giving the steelhead a fighting chance to the ultimate. Instead of using tackle which would ordinarily be deemed suitable for the taming of a fish which, pound for pound, has more energy than a grizzly, he arms himself with a five-ounce fly rod, a twelve-pound test line, an eight-pound test leader, and an infinitesimal hook which is completely covered by a single salmon egg. He fixes his eye on a patch of water about twenty feet above a rock which splits the speeding current. He tosses out his weighted line with an expert flirt of the wrist, dropping the hook upon the precise spot aimed at, which may be sixty feet distant; then braces himself and waits for business.

The salmon egg sinks down as it approaches the rock, swirls around it, riding deep; and so comes to the steelhead, which is likewise waiting for business in the lee of the rock. The steelhead has no inhibitions but many whims. He may take the bait as gently as the touch of loving fingers, savoring the salmon egg with absent-minded relish, or he may seize it and be off with the abruptness of a stone crashing through glass. In either case the hand of an expert is required. The beginner, after that moment, has neither a fish on his line nor any line left.

The steelhead's first rush, once the tiny hook is set, is savage but brief. He is merely annoyed and disbelieving. Since he is a submarine javelin of speed and can elude any enemy in river or sea, and knows it, fear is not in him. It is when he realizes that he is fighting a persistently hostile force that his full explosive fury is aroused. From that point on, for thirty crowded minutes or more, the steelhead expert tastes the kind of battle and the thrills known only to his seasoned guild.

The steelhead is upstream and down, and almost simultaneously. He is twenty feet below the surface, flashing between the darkened boulders, or five feet in the air, shaking with spleen: silvery, heavy-bodied, yet incomparably graceful and streamlined. The moment he strikes the water the reel sings. His stamina seems inexhaustible.

Finally, when the fisherman is on the verge of collapse from the furious concentration and the instant reflexes necessary to keep his gossamerlike line taut, the gallant battler dies hard. He is reeled in to twenty feet distant, seemingly done for, and explodes again. At ten feet, and five, up to the very instant the landing net encircles him or the gaff touches his spent body—or the superexpert, disdaining either net or gaff, grasps him by the gill openings with trembling fingers —he still lashes out in expiring frenzy, unyielding and indomitable to the end.

For the neophyte with steelhead ambitions such refinements of technique are out of the question. He takes a heavy rod and stout line and hook and hopes only for a strike. Sooner or later he will have a strike, and many strikes; and his ambition thereafter is actually to land a steelhead. He will hook many before he achieves it. Once he has landed his steelhead he is a confirmed addict; all the varied fishing boasted by the streams rooted in the Cascades—and in many cases, like the steelhead, peculiar to those streams—leave him unmoved. He has tasted the strong meat.

On up the Cascades, to the Canadian border and beyond, there are devotees of scores of rivers and streams who listen to steelhead stories with tolerant compassion. They call them "one-fish maniacs," due to the legend that the steelhead fisherman considers the landing of a single battler as a sufficient and crowning climax to a day's outing; and point to their own limit catches to prove that the truly peerless fishing streams are found only in the northern foothills of the range.

The salmon fisherman, on his part, views the whole field of fly-rod addicts with jaundiced amusement. *His* sport, so he believes, is king of all; and to ask him to stoop to trout fishing, except as a necessary time killer between salmon runs, is like expecting a hunter of grizzlies to spend a blood-stirring afternoon snaring bullfrogs. His quarry is appropriately called the Royal Chinook salmon, a truly regal fish almost exclusively taken in the Columbia and its Cascade-born tributaries, including the Willamette. Nine tenths of the world's supply of this premier edible fish are caught in the Columbia. It is one of Oregon's most important industries, almost a century old. The value of the annual catch runs high into the millions, and many federal and state laws are designed to protect and perpetuate the supply which comes up each year in enormous volume from the sea.

The commercial aspect of salmon fishing is another story. Within the industry it is a livelihood for thousands, and when the mighty run converges on the Columbia the silvery giants are first intercepted by a fleet of trollers which takes them literally by the ton. Once inside the river, gill nets and purse seines take their toll, and on upstream there are other nets and fish wheels and fleets of trollers. Countless thousands are taken in this manner, but countless thousands, having run the gantlet, fight on upriver, driven by some mysterious urge as inexorable and immutable as the laws of time and tide; up increasingly swift water, up man-made fish ladders and savage waterfalls, higher and farther inland, perhaps a thousand miles from the chill and silent deeps of the ocean, they come at last to their home waters, to the sluggish pool in the lee of a sand bar, or the sheltered nook under an overhanging, grassy bank. Here, as fingerlings, they began their eager flight to the sea four years before; and here, wearily, their life cycle over, their matchless stamina utterly spent and their once near-perfect bodies bruised and shredded by the teeth of the rapids, they spawn and die.

Perhaps, dimly, the king salmon brings that fatalistic knowledge with him when he comes in from the sea. Certainly he is gripped by a species of fighting madness from the moment he enters the Columbia. His far wanderings in the oceans of the hemisphere[1] have given him reserves of strength and stamina far beyond his day-to-day needs, in preparation for his last battle; and he is prepared to use them all. He has but one consuming urge—to reach the spawning ground—and nothing within the limits of his marvelous resources can deter him from it.

Once he leaves salt water he never eats again. Why he strikes at a spoon or spinner which chances to waver in his path is unknown. It is thought that the silvery flash of the spoon annoys him. He will not turn aside to strike at it, but when it does not give ground before his onward rush he snaps at it truculently in passing. Expert anglers accordingly study the contours of the river bottom and the swing of the

[1]Marked Royal Chinook have been caught off the Atlantic Coast, eleven thousand sea miles from the mouth of the Columbia.

currents so that their lures flash along the traffic lanes followed by the hidden hordes.

When the king salmon strikes the action begins at once
and does not cease or slacken or even hesitate until the king
is dead. Ordinarily there are scores of anchored boats near
by. All are spectators to the battle royal, and all shout envi-
ous and sometimes profane advice. When each of two adjacent fishermen simultaneously snare a monster it becomes a
melee enlivened with snarled gear, hands injured from
smoking and fouled lines, and sometimes overturned dories.

The fury of the salmon's battle is indescribable. It is
equaled only by that of the steelhead, but many times mag-
nified. The steelhead's top weight ends in the neighborhood
of eighteen pounds, which is a mere minnow among the
Royal Chinook. His weight ranges from twenty-five to fifty
or sixty pounds and occasionally more. A few weighing
more than seventy pounds have been taken. To land one of
these aboard a dory, even after he is gaffed and expiring, is
literally a task for strong men. And when he is aboard he
must be stunned at once, with a short club kept at hand for
the purpose, or his final struggle will make a shambles of
the dory, with gear, oars, and the fisherman's lunch flying
in all directions—and sometimes a fisherman himself going
overboard in his attempt to clamp a wrestler's hold on the
dying gladiator.

The run itself is brief, a vast army speeding by. When
the vanguard of the countless millions has reached spawning
grounds high up in the Cascades, or far inland beyond the
mountains, the last of the horde is entering the Columbia. In
the eyes of its addicts the accessibility of the sport, plus its
quality, makes up for the briefness of the season. With the

notable exception of the Deschutes River, which the salmon have never ascended for some unknown reason, most tributaries of the Columbia down to the smallest stream receive their share of the annual migration. Beginning within the city limits of Portland, on the Willamette River, the height of the run sees hundreds of boats anchored at favorite spots in the eight-mile stretch ending at the Oregon City falls.

When all is said and done—referring now to the whole field of both hunting and fishing throughout the Cascades—it is the vastness of the area accessible to the average man—the beginner, the "dub," the "great unwashed"—which is of the greater importance. The expert can take care of himself, in tough company. The common man has neither the time nor inclination for superrefinements of sport. When he goes fishing he wants to catch fish, and if his clumsy efforts with the dry fly yield nothing he will turn to the spinner and finally to baiting with grasshoppers and worms. Blandly, while the fastidious expert covers his eyes and hurries away, he catches his limit, takes it home, and eats it with complete enjoyment.

For this vast majority of the Northwest's population, and the majority of the motor tourists who flood the region each normal season, the whole length of the Cascades is a fisherman's Valhalla. The nation offers no more accessible streams, no greater variety, nor stocked with gamier fish. Within two hours' drive of the main centers of population —Portland, Tacoma, Seattle, Spokane—the average man can be whipping the riffles of a mountain stream whose banks bear no visible evidence that others have paused there before.

He enjoys it thoroughly, untroubled by the knowledge

that it can't last forever; that before many years have passed this spot, too, will be crowded. If so, he'll have to move a little higher toward the peaks. He'd intended to, anyway, when he had more time. The experts said there were a lot of good creeks up yonder.

CHAPTER XXII

Unnatural History[1]

Paul bunyan left his imprint on the Cascades country. In fact he built the great mountain barrier with his own hands. The story of the sickness of Paul's blue ox belongs to another region, but the suggested remedy—the milk of the Western whale—brought Paul and his loggers and the blue ox west to the shores of the Pacific. Here they scooped out the whale corral that was later named Coos Bay and poured the hardly won milk down the throat of the dying ox. Seeing that the remedy was failing, and Babe about to expire, Paul sorrowfully went a little way north and set his men to dig a grave.

He sat down on the Blue Mountains and brooded over the western rim of the earth, and as the piles of earth were tossed up in front of him his great hands idly formed the material into a long high wall running north and south, that would forever guard the last resting place of the blue ox from cyclone and blizzard.

Part way through this task, as everybody knows, Babe

---

[1]Authors' Note: Any resemblance or relation to fact in this folklore of the Cascades is purely coincidental.

chewed up certain carboys of epsom salts and wood alcohol, and rose up snorting, to drag the bunkhouse and the great hotcake griddle off athwart Paul's barrier. He followed Babe to the eastward and got to work again without ever stopping to log off the great forests of the Pacific Northwest. The half-finished grave is Puget Sound; the barrier ridge topped by a rock here and there along its length is the Cascade Range; and the place where the hotcake griddle hit the pile of dirt is the Columbia gorge, while a convenient bed for the river was torn up across the plateau as Babe made great leaps toward Kansas. Paul had still to turn over the wooded rolling sections of Kansas so their flat undersides would thereafter be on top, and he was able to get back to the Cascades only once, when he brought the last of the blue snow out to dump it into Crater Lake. There it melted and there it still lies, incredibly and persistently blue, to this day.

But Paul's departure did not take all the mystery out of the region of the Cascades. Indeed, it opened the eyes of the natives to the fact that a great many things may be observed, especially in the way of unnatural history.

For instance the cattle pasturing on the numerous buttes of the eastward plateau are a favored breed with legs shorter on one side than the other, so they must graze around and around the hill. Progress is made in a clockwise direction. These odd cattle are morose of disposition and attack with fury, but are easily evaded if one remembers to step aside from the rush of attack. Once beyond its mark, the critter must circle the butte again before it can attack again, and since the paths wind up like a spiral, the next round is on a higher level, and the danger no longer exists. Husbandry

Ray Atkeson

THE THREE SISTERS

each higher than 10,000 feet, in the central Oregon Cascade Range–viewed across Scott Lake

Ray Atkeson

SILVER CREEK FALLS STATE PARK, OREGON
Showing one of a dozen beautiful falls on west slope of Cascades

of these cattle is simple once they are started on the butte, but the owner must be alert to slaughter them once they reach the top, else they will stay there and starve.

Most of the queer animals are native to the region, and only the observant loggers have guessed or interpreted or—rarely—seen with their own eyes the creatures they describe so vividly. There is, in the big timber west of the Cascades, the gumberoo[2] or *Megalogaster repercussus,* which is fortunately very rare, so that its presence must be guessed at from circumstantial evidence. The gumberoo lives in the huge stumps of burned-out cedars and has an enormous appetite, so colossal, in fact, as to sustain the theory that the body is hollow all over. Its tight-stretched skin has not a wrinkle or hair, and is tough and shiny like a rubber boot. No way has been found to penetrate this tough hide with weapons. Any missile, such as a cant hook, thrown at the creature, rebounds straight at the assailant; and a bullet hitting its resilient hide flies with the same speed back to crash the brains of the hunter.

The gumberoo burns with a furious force, somewhat like an old automobile tire. Whenever a forest fire sweeps a stand of giant cedars there may be heard loud reports, like the sound of falling trees, and the smell of burning rubber spurts out of the hotness; and this means that another gumberoo has gone back to the original latex from whence he sprang.

The splinter cat (*Felynx arbordiffisus*) is not perhaps a native of this area, but a few roving specimens have left their mark, in the form of trees broken or shattered high

[2] See *Fearsome Creatures of the Lumberwoods* by William T. Cox, published 1910 by Judd and Detweiler, Inc., Washington, D.C.

up the trunk, as if wrenched by a high wind. The huge square-faced flying cat is responsible for this damage. He lives on wild honey, which is to be found in dead trees where wild bees have lived, but the splinter cat is no mental giant. Instead of seeking a tree that hums like a taut wire, the big cat climbs any convenient elevation and launches himself across toward the nearest tree, smashing it off. If this tree proves to be barren of honey—as is usually the case —the odd creature simply climbs and splinters again, until at last it happens upon a store of honey or batters itself into nothingness and is known no more. Sometimes a whole terrain may bear witness to the blind hunger of a splinter cat. Such a one died in a little gully near Mount Hood, and the spot is now named Splinter Cat Creek.

East of the Cascades, in the sagebrush and jack-rabbit country, dwells the roperite or *Rhynchoropus flagelliformis*. News of this galloping nightmare is reputed to derive from the Digger Indians, themselves odd, slinking men who lived in holes. The lot of these prideless unfortunates was no whit improved by the spectacle of a roperite splitting the breeze behind a fleeing antelope and swinging its long ropelike nose for a cast at its prey.

The range of the agropelter (*Anthrocephalus craniofractens*) is along both sides of the Cascades, wherever loggers walk in the big timber. Many a logger has been killed by a falling branch, and his companions marveled that the aim of the dead wood could be so deadly until it was learned that the agropelter lives in dead treetops and has no reason for living except to heave these missiles at unwary passers-by. His arms are like whiplashes, and he can snap his dead wood at the target with the speed of a six-inch gun.

Up from the Mexican border there wandered a strange animal which—since it is virtually indestructible—must still be living near the southern end of the Cascades. This is the whintosser (*Cephalovertens semperambulatus*), a small, bitter, and unbelieving creature always out hunting for trouble. It is shaped like a triangular log, and its head and tail fasten on with swivels, while each flat surface of its body has its own set of legs. The animal may thus be tossed on its back or side and its head will swivel into place, and the four legs touching the ground immediately begin to run. The animal may be beaten, gouged, or blasted with buckshot and it lives on. The only known method of killing it is to thrust it into a flume pipe so all three sets of legs begin to operate at the same time, and the creature is torn apart.

Somewhere between fact and fiction is the lava bear, reputedly a small subspecies that lives in the area of recent lava flow near the Three Sisters. Over this incredibly rough terrain the lava bear is said to find shelter and food and to reproduce its kind. The great Irvin S. Cobb made his way to the Cascades area for the express purpose of hunting lava bears but the difficulties of the terrain were such—each place of entertainment was an almost insuperable obstacle to progress—and the eagerness of the local residents to hear his inimitable stories so strong that he never won beyond the lower fringes of the area, and the lava bear has not yet been proved or disproved.

CHAPTER XXIII

The Economic Picture

LET US CONSIDER (in resuming our factual narrative) the effect of the Cascade Range on the economy of the Northwest.

The two states cut by the great barrier boast a population about three and a half million, of whom more than 98 per cent are whites, with only a small sprinkling of Orientals, Indians, and Negroes. A large congregation of Finns at the mouth of the Columbia River, a few German, Swiss, and other communities scattered through the fertile westward valleys, and a settlement of Basque sheepherders on the inland plateau lend color to the local picture.

Two thirds of the population crowd into the narrow valleys west of the Cascades, occupying scarcely one third of the land area, and the other one third of the people scatter far and wide across the great plateau. The population density in the Willamette Valley, sheltered by the Cascades, is 45.5 per square mile; in the sun-baked counties of Harney and Lake there is an average of two people to three square miles.

In the western valleys the three great sources of income

are food production, lumbering, and industry, in that order. Many of the truck gardeners and fruit growers live on land taken out of the free wilderness by their fathers and grandfathers, but they ship their produce to peoples never even remotely known to the pioneers. Traffic follows the old roads first rutted by the oxcarts, but the thousand and one services brought to the humblest door are beyond the pioneer dreams of luxury.

The great output of hydroelectric power serves the people well. The "per user" consumption of electricity is almost twice the national average, a record that speaks eloquently of labor-saving machines and abundant light. A larger percentage of farms in this area is served by electricity than in any other part of the nation.

On one side stretch the shores of the Pacific Ocean, waiting for the leisure week end; and on the other the forest-clad slopes of the Cascades lead upward to the snow fields. Record per-acre production of truck crops, world's records in egg laying and milk production, an abundance of harvest that includes every variety of fruit and vegetable possible to grow in the Temperate Zone, produce an effect like some giant horn of plenty spilled along the highways.

It is difficult to exaggerate the place of the Cascades in this economy. Sheltering the area from the extremes of continental weather, the mountains permit the moderate winters and long growing season that make this area immensely successful in every aspect of living. Catching and storing a huge snowfall, the mountains again deliver the water to keep the area green, carry on their slopes the forests that will supply timber in perpetuity, and make possible the development of hydroelectric power that will someday astound the world.

Food processing and wood-products manufacturing account for about three fourths of the manufacturing employment in normal times. The pressure of war needs pushed shipbuilding temporarily into first place, and brought airplane manufacture into third place. War pressure, too, taking advantage of the large supplies of power available, has thrust forward development in electrochemical and metallurgical fields. Still manufacture here is largely concerned with processing and fabricating native raw materials, and this will probably continue to be the field in which development occurs after the war, since there is still so much room for expansion. The process of general manufacture of materials imported from other areas will probably await some future day.

Across the Cascade Range, less than an hour's drive away, is the vast broken plateau, shaded from rain, subject to extreme heat and bitter cold, and carrying only one third of the population of the two states. Some of these people are collected into urban centers of trade, some gathered about the irrigated areas, and some ride alone with no other habitation from one edge of the horizon to the other. Here are wheat fields that disappear over the curve of the earth, vast herds of cattle, great bands of sheep that, moving, seem to be an undulation of the crust of the earth. Here, wherever water can be brought to the soil, there springs up richness of orchard and field crop. But water can be brought by gravity flow to only a small percentage of the vast broken plateau. Rivers have cut deep ravines, and some means must be devised to raise this water to the land level. Here again the Cascade Range offers the answer. Before history was written the Cascades formed this plateau out of white-hot hearts; now the mountains offer the water to moisten the land, and tumbling streams to create hydroelectric power to pump the water upon the land.

To the cattle and sheep men the Cascades furnish another great boon, the one consideration that makes the great arid range country usable. Stock may be kept on the open range during the winter, with their grazing supplemented by alfalfa from the bottom lands, but the long summer would prove their undoing, except that the near-by slopes of the Cascades offer the ideal summer pasture amid the pine forests. Here the grass springs up in the melting snow, and sheep and cattle pasture in abundance, climbing ever higher as the summer waxes, until they can descend in the autumn to the new grass on the range. The presence of these mountain pastures permits utilization of two million acres of range land that would otherwise suffice for only a handful of stock.

The economy of the region is unbalanced—an overproduction of food, an underproduction of manufactured commodities. If this Cascades area were somehow cut off from outside imports the picture would at once be clear. The food stores would be virtually unchanged, with their shelves and frozen-food lockers still crammed to bursting with vegetables and fruit of all kinds, fresh, preserved, canned, and frozen, to include everything except citrus fruits and such items as pineapples, bananas, and coconuts. The meat markets would be hung with beef, pork, and mutton, and the choicest of fish and seafoods would be there in abundance. Turkeys, chickens, eggs, milk, butter, cheese would be available far beyond the capacity of the region to consume, for this area furnishes, in addition to its own needs, food enough to serve three meals a day, the year around, to five million people. There would be beet sugar and honey and walnuts and fruit-flavored desserts for which the world would yearn.

The gardens, too, would be rich with flowers—iris, daffodils, regal lilies, tulips, peonies, roses, chrysanthemums—for this area has established a huge industry in bulbs and cuttings. The native-grass lawns about the frame houses would be edged with a variety of shrubs. The area would be embarrassed by the wealth of vegetable seed, flower seed, and seed grains.

The houses would be built from foundation to roof from material cut and processed in the area, but there would be no nails, no tools, no equipment. The floors would be bare and the furniture without upholstery, for there is no weaving of tapestries here. There might be kitchen stoves and furnaces, but no other kitchen equipment, with the exception of an occasional pottery dish or "hotel china" plate.

The resident might dress himself in a bathing suit that is the choice of the beaches of the world, or don a wool outer garment from local mills, or wrap himself in one of the finest blankets in the nation, but his cotton and silk and linen needs must go unsatisfied.

He would be without machinery, automobiles, or any other means of transportation, except for his horse and saddle. His education could be carried into the most highly specialized research, except that equipment would be missing. However, if he became ill, he could draw on the nation's supply of cascara, a good output of digitalis, an abundance of Vitamin A, and a nice supply of the Chinese herb ginseng.

He would have music, poetry, and art, and his literature would be abundant at least, and supplied with plenty of wood-pulp paper for printing. Concrete products and explosives would serve his needs, but the luxury goods, the newest products of the machines, and the machines themselves, would not be there.

In short the area is rich in raw materials and has a possibility for great expansion in these fields. Agriculture has a good future, with scarcely one fifth of the available land developed; lumbering is already a great industry, and open to indefinite expansion along processing lines. Ores are cheap and abundant, but manufacturing has not yet established itself. What will emerge from the war-encouraged production of electric power, along with industrial workers brought into the area to serve wartime needs, is a question that cannot be answered yet.

CHAPTER XXIV

Character of the People

Each region draws its own kind and in turn molds the minds and characters of those whom it draws. Nowhere can such a thesis be established as readily as in the Cascades country. The mountain barrier divides the two states into areas of almost opposite climates and thus decides the natural conditions under which the people live; the people themselves seem peculiarly fitted to the area.

There was no necessity for conquest in the lush seaward valleys. Once the pioneers won their way across the continent and descended the western slopes of the Cascades there was no further danger from the Indians nor the climate. They could settle themselves to till the land, log the forest, establish a permanent government, and build a comfortable and aesthetically satisfying life.

With this forceful and self-reliant group suddenly freed from the actual fight for existence, it was inevitable that the nation should feel the impact of their response.

The first effects of the Oregon settlement and the Oregon demand for membership in the United States of America was a stretching of the national imagination. Settlers on the

East coast had made their bid for a place in history in 1776, but the possibility of expanding this empire was remote. They clung to the eastern fringe of the continent, promising the Indians they would never be disturbed if they withdrew across the Mississippi, and they set themselves to win, if they could, some kind of recognition among the nations of the world. Now, suddenly, scarcely seventy years later, came a group crossing three thousand miles of continent, establishing homes, and demanding that the precariously organized group of colonies extend a wing to cover them. A wing that stretched across a continent must inevitably shelter the land between, and this would mean a national empire almost beyond credulity.

A reading of contemporary discussion will indicate what a tremendous impact the Oregon demand for recognition made on Congress. Suddenly the new United States of America had expanded across the continent; suddenly here was a foothold on the vast uncharted Pacific Ocean; suddenly the fabulously powerful British Empire must be met and contested with, in the period of her greatest colonization. And most incredible of all, the American Government, precariously organized, scarcely understood, operating only indifferently well, and strongly suspected by the elder statesmen of being impractical, was actually chosen and demanded by free men; and these free men were men so simple and direct that no politician could understand them, so determined that they would cross the continent to lay their demands before Congress, so convinced that the system of democratic government was the best possible system that they put aside the proffered British rule, ignored the possibility of forming their own republic, and came back home to be recognized.

With new-found courage, with faith reaffirmed, the nation moved to accept the Oregon Territory; made a beginning at the Indian problem with the aim, for the first time, of throwing the whole continent open to white settlement; accepted at last in their imaginations the import of the Louisiana Purchase; took over California and looked toward a boundary with Mexico, and even, incredibly, acceded to the purchase of the vast unknown land of Alaska.

In many ways, minor and major, the peculiar quality of the people of the Cascades area has made itself felt. It was the Oregon settlers who devised and voted the "initiative and referendum" measures that brings government directly to the people by providing that measures passed by the state legislature may be submitted, on demand, to popular vote, and—more important still—made it possible for popularly conceived measures to become law without the aid of the legislature. It was Oregon that solved the problem of good roads for automobiles by the incredibly simple method of taxing gasoline and using the proceeds to build roads—a method copied by every state in the Union as soon as their first gasp of surprise was over.

It was in the Cascades area that Indians were first gathered into reservations, that great reaches of timber were first set aside as national forest reserves. This area pioneered rural public health organization and developed the quick freezing of foods to the status of an industry.

Oregon pioneers had time for education, and they established a scattering of small colleges throughout the area, so that the percentage of literacy is one of the highest in the roll of states. Oregon must have good health, and the child mortality rate is the lowest on record.

The struggle in the beginning, west of the Cascades, was to make the rest of the nation believe the stories that derived from Oregon. Oregon grain, vegetables, and fruits were so large and richly colored as to arouse suspicion of their authenticity. Letters written "home" evoked roars of incredulous merriment over the idea that cherries might be as large as plums, plums larger than peaches, peaches surpass apples, and the apples outweigh melons.

Joseph Watt, settled on a donation land claim in the Willamette Valley, persuaded his neighbors to join him in sending a shipload of Oregon wheat to the New York market. The large white grains would surely bring a premium.

The ship journeyed around Cape Horn and reached New York; the incredulous buyers consulted a miller, and he gave as his considered opinion that the wheat had become damp on the way and had swollen to this unusual size. Instead of a premium, the cargo netted a loss of eight thousand dollars. Nevertheless another year saw a shipload of wheat going out to Liverpool, England, and this time there was a profit, and the vast shipment of agricultural products from this area was under way.

Adventure in the westward valleys is a matter of imagination rather than of actual physical contests. The story of Opal Whitely is a case in point.

Opal was reared in a small town near the western foothills of the Cascades and was ostensibly one of the children of a local logger. She was not distinguished except by an odd elfin charm and a fervent imagination. She entered the

University of Oregon and still nothing indicated that she would presently arouse a national controversy that would racket from one ocean to the other.

She found her way to Boston, after a year at college, and entered the editorial offices of the *Atlantic Monthly*, where she divulged shyly to the late editor, Ellery Sedgwick, that she was not what she seemed but actually was a princess. Her book, *The Diary of an Understanding Heart*, was written, she said, when she was four and five years old, and had been kept secret from her family and friends until this moment. She presented various scraps of paper covered with a round, childish hand. Mr. Sedgwick found real literary merit in the writing and was charmed and convinced by her story of her romantic origin. He encouraged her to recopy the diary and present it for publication, and presently the astounded literati of the nation learned that this charming elfin child was actually a daughter of a member of the French house of Orleans, with some claim still pending on the throne of France; and her mother (the marriage was never made public, she said) was a maiden of Hindu birth, sister, in short, of one of the most comfortably situated rajahs then enjoying the protection of the British. Little anecdotes set down in touching detail, great affairs hinted at, a hovering of mystery and pathos, a knowledge of the stories of the classics far beyond the normal range of a logger's child added an air of verisimilitude to the narrative. It is a tribute to Opal's personality that the eminent editor did not remember that the average child in a low-income family has little privacy and cannot hide as much as a postal card over the years without detection, while Opal's diary must have filled two bushel baskets. Similarly it is difficult to introduce a child of exotic parentage into the ordinary fish bowl of small-town life without some outside comment.

Heated controversy raged from the slopes of the Cascades —where Opal's neighbors lived—up through the centers of literature and international diplomacy, and indeed the temperature rose inside the office of the somewhat crest-fallen Mr. Sedgwick. Eventually he withdrew his sponsor-ship and Opal Whitely dropped from sight. Not much more has been heard about her, except for a story that came back to her home town around 1928. An Oregon woman, ac-quainted personally with Opal Whitely in her home com-munity, was traveling in India. Her conveyance drew aside to permit passage of a company of mounted native soldiers, conveying a carriage of the type used by royalty. The at-tendants were richly decked and suspicious of curious eyes, but the curtains of the carriage swung aside for a moment, and out of the gleam of silks and jewels looked the familiar elfin face of Opal Whitely. The last chapter in this odd story has not been written, and the last word will not have been said until the final survivor among Opal's contempo-raries has reached the grave.

History made some slight mark on this placid western valley. Captain Philip Sheridan built a fort or two and ruled the beggarly Indians on the first reservations, meanwhile climbing daily to the nearest hilltop to watch for a rider who might bring orders calling him back home to engage in the Civil War. Ulysses S. Grant was an officer at Fort Van-couver until he grew weary of separation from his family. William Henry Seward traveled north from California along this route to take his first look at newly purchased Alaska; but mostly the storms of conflict passed the area by.

East of the Cascades the picture is far different. The endless grazing lands and flat wheat fields had to be won by sheer rawhide courage. Exceedingly agile Indians were wont to swoop down on unwary homesteaders and burn house and corral, drive off the cattle, and kill whatever human beings they could find. Not until the discovery of gold in this area was there a determined effort to subdue the Indians and travel the vast plateau; and only the demands for food of the gold seekers forced development of the cattle industry.

Then great cattle ranches were established and their influence lingers today in this area that is eminently suited to cattle and sheep raising. John Devine rode into Harney County on a prancing white horse, himself trapped out like a Spanish don. Through means ethical and otherwise he acquired title to a hundred and fifty thousand acres of grazing land; and so rich was the reward that when his patents were declared illegal, and the land opened again for homesteading, he was able to buy the land over again from the new settlers. He was driven to bankruptcy by an arid spell, and the man who took over his holdings declined to fence him in on a city lot, but presented him with six thousand acres upon which to spend his declining years.

Henry Miller and his partners accumulated about a million acres of land and more than a million head of cattle; Peter French entered the Blitzen Valley and found a wild meadow stretching for seventy miles along the river. Here he established his empire and fought Indians, sheepmen, and homesteaders, until a neighbor caught him off guard and ended the story with a shotgun.

William Hanley was one of the most colorful and public-

FALLS ON THE McKENZIE RIVER, OREGON

A part of the billions of tons of melted snow that pours annually
to the sea

MOUNT JEFFERSON FROM JEFFERSON PARK
The Cascades' most difficult peak to scale

spirited of the old-time cattle barons and also one of the most durable. He still owned his 17,000-acre cattle ranch when he died in 1935, and many famous people wended their way up the eight-mile "front walk" from his gate to his door.

Here a man may still ride his horse from dawn until dusk without seeing another human being; here a town of six thousand is a highly organized and influential city; here the urban center of thousands of square miles may have located inside its city limits an authentic and entirely casual Indian village; here a single man with a post office can incorporate a "one-man" town and put himself on the map.

A cloudburst may still turn up skeletons from a dry wash, and local gossip will tell the story of a sheepman who engaged herders to tend his sheep all year and "paid" them at the end with a shotgun, laying them away in peace under the near-by gravel.

They travel across the Cascades and descend the western slopes, these people of the high country, to visit Portland on the Willamette River and Seattle and her sister cities on Puget Sound. The trip across the range takes perhaps an hour by automobile, a few minutes by airplane. They take their sons and daughters to the state university, transact business at the industrial centers, hear the symphony orchestra and see the latest theater productions, visit the style shops and the automobile show and the state fair, deck themselves in silks and furs for a night at the Pacific International Horse Show, and loll for a few days by the ocean. Then they flee gratefully back across the narrow mountain barrier to their own beloved sand and sagebrush and give thanks that they have escaped from the oppressive comfort of the lower valley.

And over from the valley, each summer, flows a steady stream of hunters, fishermen, and vacationists, bound for the high desert, to gaze awesomely at the bare bones of the earth, a sight rare indeed in the deeply foliaged valley. They ride horses and fill their lungs with dry, clean air; they gather semiprecious stones from the range country and marvel over the story of the ages in the "picture rocks." They visit the ice caves, the underground lava channels, the myriad mysteries and beauties of the range country; they look once again at the far horizon unsmudged by smoke or sign of human habitation, and they view the marching snow peaks from the "other side" with a new wonder. Then they turn back gratefully across the Cascades to settle down in their homes again. And the great barrier of the Cascades, at once a barrier and a retaining wall, a divider and a tie that binds the two regions together, looks down benignly on the varied lands under its rule.

CHAPTER XXV

Rose Festival

No SINGLE INSTANCE will point the contrast in life and character wrought by the Cascades as clearly as a description of the two nationally known celebrations held in this area each year.

The Portland Rose Festival, staged in the metropolis of the Willamette Valley each June, typifies the people and the kind of life they lead; and the Pendleton Roundup, held scarcely two hundred miles away across the barrier of the Cascades, in its turn is a natural product of the area, expressing the life and nature of the people.

The Rose Festival is a public celebration, staged for the public with no thought of profit nor any purpose except to spill out a lavish display of blooms, here where roses bloom in the parkings and about the lawns, and deck with equally perfect bloom the garden of professional or amateur.

The celebration dates back forty-five years to the first rose show held by the Portland Rose Society in 1889. For a year or two the show was enough. Then the Society arranged a floral parade through downtown streets of Portland in 1904. The decorated carriages, bicycles, and horses were joined by four automobiles that moved precariously and stopped so often that the crowds rocked with merriment. Stung by this ridicule, the automobile owners gathered their forces and staged a second parade a few days later, with the astounding number of twenty automobiles in line, all decorated and all actually moving. From this beginning the festival expanded, with the parade as the backbone, and whatever other events occurred to the committee from time to time. One year trolley cars might range the streets, laden with roses to scatter through the crowds; another time the Navy would send several cruisers and torpedo boats up into the river that cuts through the heart of the city, and make the night sky brilliant with searchlights, while the personnel flocked into every event. Always there is a rose show. The original ruler, the fat and jolly "King Rex Oreganus," and his consort "Queen Flora" gave way, in recent years, to a queen and court chosen from the high school girls of the city. One year the featured event was a musical pageant with a chorus one thousand strong; another year an electrical parade at night featured "The Spirit of the Golden West."

The usual schedule for the Rose Festival occupies three days. First the princesses are chosen, one senior girl from each high school, with each beautiful princess "owning" the daily newspapers for the day. From this group the queen is chosen, and the others form her court. During this interval the Rose Festival committee stages a sale of tags or buttons, each of which admits the wearer to a reserved seat in the outdoor stadium where the parade forms. This is the only commercial aspect of the Festival and is no restriction whatever of full enjoyment of the spectacle, for the parade leaves the stadium and winds for miles through the city streets, where all may witness it. Proceeds from the seat sale meet the expenses of the Rose Festival and provide prizes for the entries in the parade.

Once the queen is chosen, and her princesses robed to rival Cinderella at the ball, a guard of honor is formed from the white-uniformed rose-emblemed knights of Rosaria. About the city they go, touring hospitals, appearing at the rose show, lending a kindly sponsorship to the juvenile "junior festival" in one of the city parks, and finally taking their places in the royal float to enter the parade.

The parade is the true Rose Festival. Portland loves a parade. Thousands of spectators in holiday best fill the stadium, and other thousands gather along the downtown parade route, sitting along the curb on boxes, filling porches and windows, moving, flowing, collecting children and losing them again, in cheerful anticipation that will presently mount to wild excitement. Presently a band is heard, and the roars of cheering swell up closer and closer, and at long last the parade moves slowly into view. It may be five miles long, but the spectators are out to make a day of it and will be there cheering as loudly for the last entry as the first.

The main body of the parade is made up of floats, which are automobiles or trucks disguised completely, even to their wheels, with flowers. One may be in the form of a swan, another a basket of flowers, another the artful depiction of a peacock with his tail folding and unfolding as he moves along the street. Story floats are frequent, with scenes from pioneer life, a model of the big Bonneville Dam, replica of Mount Hood, the dashing surf of a seaside resort, all built from flowers, and all, of course, decorated with Portland's best skill, and topped by another sample of the wealth of the region—healthy and well-formed youth. Spaced along the parade line are lodge bands, high school bands, military and naval bands, visiting Scottish bands, girls' bands, Hawaiian groups, to furnish the marching music. From time to time come the marching units formed by near-by towns especially for this occasion, each group in its own uniform, drilling and forming squads and wheeling and turning, staging a special bit of fancy drilling when the parade stops, turning back into line again when the signal comes to move on. A detachment of Mounted Police may be down from Canada in red tunics and broad hats, a visiting "sheriff's posse" on matched horses up from California.

Floats are built and decorated by business houses, fraternal organizations, near-by communities, and individuals competing for the coveted ribbons that reward their ingenuity and taste.

There is a tradition that no artificial flowers may be used in a Rose Festival parade, and the onlooker does well to remind himself of this fact; otherwise he might not believe that the gardens of the entire state could yield so many blooms.

CHAPTER XXVI

Pendleton Roundup

THE PENDLETON ROUNDUP, staged at Pendleton, Oregon, in the heart of the eastern plateau, is also a non-profit organization, with the immense "take" devoted to offering ever larger prizes for the world's championship events, and any surplus money spread around to beautify the city of Pendleton.

The Roundup derived, in a way, from the Rose Festival. Around 1910 a number of Pendleton citizens were down, as usual, to see the roses and the parade. They happened to gather at lunch, and someone suggested that Pendleton might have some community celebration. It wouldn't, of course, be a flower show, but something akin to the rough, action-packed work of the cattle ranges. Top hands from neighboring ranches would be invited to compete in riding, calf roping, and racing. It would be a good thing for Pendleton—advertise the town, bring people in, encourage business.

The first Roundup was held in a corral, with the visitors crowded around to perch on the railing. One feature that won approval was an Indian dance put on by some bucks from the Umatilla Reservation. It proved to be a nice variation in the program and gave the cow hands a bit of time to rest between spills from the bucking horses. The next year the corral fence disappeared entirely under the crowd, and half the visitors couldn't see the events, so the committee had to plan a grandstand and bleachers for the next year. They prepared seats for fifteen thousand people and felt a little abashed when they saw the vast spread of seats. Maybe they were too hopeful. It might take ten years to pay off the cost of the grandstand. But when the Roundup opened it seemed as if the whole country had moved into Pendleton, and the committee had to consider an even larger grandstand for the next year.

They formed the Northwest Frontier Exhibition Association, sold shares at ten dollars each to raise money, and set up seats for twenty-five thousand people. The city of Pendleton numbers around six thousand, and a crowd of this size fills all of the ordinary lodgings and forces every householder to fight off the "friends" who come to look him up at Roundup time. The railroad must run special trains and keep them on the sidings throughout the affair, to furnish beds and meals to their passengers. Every man in town must volunteer to direct traffic, police the grounds, marshal the parade, procure livestock and tend it, announce the events, handle the ticket sales, and play host to the visitors. And merrily do the citizenry of Pendleton respond. Garbed in "ten-gallon" hats, neckcloths, high-heeled boots, and shirts to rival the rainbow, they put aside their normal pursuits and engage in a great three-day jamboree. Two of the committee's aims are realized: the city of Pendleton is advertised, rather more widely than they anticipated; and "people are encouraged to come in" but there isn't any time for ordinary business.

With this initial burgeoning of the Roundup, there came a critical time for the great celebration. A New York concern wired an offer for all of the stock of the corporation, quoting a price of fifty dollars a share, and promising to make the Roundup the biggest affair of its kind in the entire West.

The decision was not arrived at easily; but out of the welter of argument it developed that most of the stockholders wanted to keep the affair in local hands as a community enterprise. Now they regretted that they had incorporated, for outsiders were already bidding up the shares and might in time pick up enough to gain control. By this time the corporation owned the Roundup grounds and stands, a string of good buckers, and considerable "property" in the form of old stagecoaches, covered wagons, and various whatnots used in the pioneer parades.

A suggestion was made and voted down; reiterated, discussed, and thrown out; brought up again and finally voted through. The corporation would deed to the city of Pendleton the entire Roundup park, under an arrangement whereby it could be rented back at a nominal price each year. This stripped the corporation shares of their cash value. Now nobody would be tempted to buy the stock, since it had only a voting value, and there would be no way of taking the control of the Roundup out of local hands. This proved to be true, except that the stock is quoted at fifty dollars a share, the same price offered as almost irresistible bait by the New York concern. There is no return on the investment, no distribution of profits, no actual property there to justify such a price, but Pendleton citizens have bid up the stock for the pure joy of belonging to the corporation.

The Pendleton Roundup is widely known. Cowboys come from the entire West, including Canada and Mexico, to compete for world-championship status, and the cow hands from the stock ranches of the Pendleton area come in to try themselves out against the big boys. Many a rodeo career has begun—and many ended—at Pendleton; many a movie hero got his first start toward the Western films in this dusty arena.

Between each championship event—Brahma steer riding, calf roping, relay race, bulldogging, pony express race, and the bucking contests—comes an amateur event, or a non-competitive bit of action, such as milking a wild cow, riding a wild horse bareback, stagecoach race, or the Roundup "derby" in which the cow hands race their own work ponies. Through the program stalk the colorful figures of the Indians.

The Indian display is conceded to be the most spectacular staged anywhere. Part of its character derives from the fact that the Indians are actually natives of the area, living on near-by reservations—Nez Perce, Umatilla, Walla Walla, Cayuse, and Yakima—and they wear garments and regalia actually worn by their forefathers. Their war whoops and yells would have sent the grandfathers of the present audience clutching for their guns in dead earnest. The rest of the success of the Indian pageant is due to the building up of this part of the program, the careful collection of clothing and feathered headdress, the many hours spent by the Indian youths in perfecting the tribal dances, and the eagerness with which the Indians look forward to this annual affair.

The result is a somewhat glorified authenticity. Where once the Indian chief must earn each separate feather in his headdress by a separate deed of valor, now everybody, old and young, wears feathers and even a feathered war bonnet. Once the papooses might have appeared naked in such a parade; now they wear the full regalia of a hero of the tribes. The Indian dress loses nothing by this encouragement to display. Buckskin garments, once the everyday wear of these tribes, are now one and all beaded and fringed and decorated with quills. The tribes have added gantlets, decorated wands and tomahawks, shawls and belts and moccasins, until the whole display is colorful beyond the ordinary and somehow moving to the emotions.

Each afternoon for three days the program is packed with action in the arena, with a new event waiting and ready before the previous one is finished. Each night the Indians stage a pageant in the arena, and following this the crowds make their way to "Happy Canyon"—a dance hall on the grounds—set up to simulate an old-time gambling hell. Here the bar is a hundred feet long, the painted ladies are back again, and the roulette wheels, faro tables, and other gambling devices are in full swing, all played with synthetic money known as "Roundup bucks."

The three-day show is more than a mere exhibition. Its outward aspect is that of a glorified and exceedingly robust circus, but its significance is rooted deeply in the locale and the temperament of its people. The hair-raising contests within the arena merely demonstrate, in near-perfect technique, the workaday chores going forward on scores of ranches on the eastern slopes and plateaus of the range. The Indian parade is more than a spectacle; the grandfathers of these painted braves, and the grandfathers of many of those who watch, once fought for possession of the ground over which the parade passes. It is, therefore, history recreated as well as a pageant dedicated to and exemplifying the primitive and colorful drama of the living stage.

CHAPTER XXVII

Whiskey Gulch

THE INFLUENCE of early-day gold mining is still felt in the brakes and plateaus extending eastward from the Cascades. Though most of the original placer ground has long since been worked out, a few dredges are still uprooting the sand flats and peaceful sod in occasional corners of the John Day valley.

Its history lives on. Some of the factual background of the region has a flavor nostalgic to Bret Harte enthusiasts of a generation ago. The staking of the discovery claim in "Whiskey Gulch" in the early sixties, for example, ushered in a "boom town" chapter as spectacular as any recorded by the inimitable author of *The Outcasts of Poker Flat*.

News of the Whiskey Gulch strike—perhaps the greatest single placer gold discovery during the half century between the California and Klondike bonanzas—permeated the wilderness like wildfire. Overnight, almost, a roaring metropolis sprung up along the banks of a creek which thrust briefly into the timbered ridges south of the main valley. At its peak the "shack town" paralleling the creek was two miles long and two houses wide, and boasted a population of six thousand. When the diggings failed the bulk of this wilderness army melted away, seeking new fields. A few remained; and upon the ruins of Whiskey Gulch was built the thriving town of today: Canyon City, county seat of Grant County, Oregon, and the trading center for a great livestock empire.

A few of the ancient buildings still front on the main street of Canyon City. One of these historic structures—whose erection in Whiskey Gulch was accompanied by events typical of both times and men—is the First Methodist Episcopal Church of Canyon City.

In the decade following the staking of the discovery claim citizens of Whiskey Gulch had little time to ponder over matters spiritual. At the peak of the excitement gold was being taken from the ground at the rate of a million dollars a month. Much of this was immediately put into circulation, with the result that the Gulch became famous throughout the wilderness as a genial metropolis where those who desired action on their money could get it; where personal liberty was defined by the individual, and the .44 Colt was king.

For prospectors who had known profitless months and years in the lonely wilds the Gulch must have presented a species of material Valhalla. Each shovelful of gravel, in the rich claims, panned out an average day's wage. Within a stone's throw of the claim boundaries were palaces of amusement, refreshment, and chance. The treasure chest seemed exhaustless; and the ancient fact of human frailty decrees that the memory of barren years must bow before the bead on a brimming glass, the lilting music of a woman's laugh, or the droning voice of the dealer calling the bets as placed.

In that first highly interesting interval, therefore, the economic life of the region proceeded as a species of twenty-four-hour shift. By day thousands toiled in the stream bed and on the rocky slopes. By night the Gulch was ablaze with light, noisy with laughter and song, the sweating routine of the day and other yesterdays and inevitable tomorrows alike forgotten.

But changes came quickly. The genial toilers of the Gulch awoke one morning to find a citizens' committee formed for the dispensing of justice. This marked the passing of an ancient order and the ushering in of the new. Hardly had the citizens' committee become accepted as an institution before it was replaced by a legally constituted court, with further definitions of justice and restrictions of personal liberty. Then came schools, the incorporation of the town, the forming of the county—all monuments to the crumbling of an old regime.

Lastly came Preacher Todd, who built a church.

Whiskey Gulch was ready for each of these epochal changes, but did not know it. Each was logical, inevitable. A law of social progress decrees that when the need arises the remedy is forthcoming. Yet the creation of the citizens' committee, the court, the regularly constituted county government, were greeted with surprise, for the need of these things was but a vague ferment in the consciousness of thinking men.

It was so, too, in matters spiritual. The need was there; but at first blush the idea was bizarre indeed. Thus the arrival of Preacher Todd, a slight, frail person, with the eyes of a dreamer and a fighting jaw, together with his calm announcement as he dismounted from his decrepit pony in front of the Lucky Strike to the effect that he proposed to build a church in Whiskey Gulch, was greeted with general and sardonic disbelief.

Within twenty-four hours after his arrival their amusement became tinged with tolerance and respect. Action, in the frontier, was rated far above words; and Preacher Todd, it developed, said little but worked fast.

It chanced that a livery stable on the main street, operated by Poole Brothers, who were also the proprietors of the Lucky Strike palace of gin and chance, and the Blue Mountain Hotel, had burned to the ground some two weeks before. On the day after his arrival Preacher Todd was seen industriously digging in the smoke-blackened ruins. Upon inquiry it developed that the brothers Poole, who as good gamblers were not averse to staking a losing player, had donated the site with the specific understanding that a church should be constructed thereon.

"This church business," said bulky Homer Poole, "isn't helping our business any, but it's liable to better someone's hand. This admittedly is one sinful community. Moreover, business is poor. Maybe ante-ing for the opposition will change our luck."

Fronting on the street, Preacher Todd erected a sign before which curious citizens paused. It read:

UPON THIS SITE

*With the help of the Almighty and
the citizens of Whiskey Gulch,
will be erected*

A CHURCH

The following contributions are hereby
acknowledged:

1. Rev. Joel H. Todd......................His life
2. Poole Bros...........................This site
3. Applejack Jim $20

There was something impressive in this brief inscription. Beyond the sign, as the curious ones read, the preacher labored, saying nothing, clearing the blackened debris. He had dedicated his life. He was toiling with his hands. These facts could not be laughed away.

There was also something unbelievable. It was the name of Applejack, a notorious person given to strong liquor and riotous living, whose name was first and last in the list of cash contributors.

They sought out Applejack, who leaned on his shovel and regarded his questioners with a furtive, watery eye. His hands were shaking, and he licked his parched lips as he talked; but he was sober. His words were not irreverent, and in his voice was a species of dejected amazement.

"I've got religion, folks," he announced. "I'm hopin' to hold out till night.

"It happened to me this-a-way. Havin' come to at the usual time this morning, I was bearin' toward the Lucky Strike for a eye opener, when this reverend fixes them eagle eyes on me. I comes to a halt, and he says: 'Brother, you passed by here last night. You were drunk.'

" 'I don't doubt it, Reverend,' I says. 'Whereas the milestones in my sinful life ain't markin' the times I'm drunk, but when I'm sober.'

" 'As you passed by,' he continues, 'you gave me this twenty-dollar gold piece.' And he holds it out.

" 'Keep it,' I says. 'I don't recall sittin' in on the deal, but since I've placed my bets we'll just leave it lay.'

" 'I'll call and raise,' says the reverend, who seems to know his poker. 'I'll keep this for the church fund, on one condition.'

" 'I'll see your raise,' I says. 'Name it.'

" 'As long as you stay sober,' he says, 'your name heads the list of cash contributors. This money will help lay the foundation stones of the church. The first time you're drunk I'll return it to you and your name will be stricken from the roll.'

" 'Listen,' I says, after thinking this over. 'Leave me duck into the Lucky Strike for my eye opener. One more little snort won't do any harm. After that we'll talk business.'

" 'No,' he says, real gentle and firm. 'It's now or never, Applejack Jim.'

"So, folks"—Applejack eyed his audience with gloomy pride—"I ain't had no morning's morning, nor no nooner, nor nothin'. I'm so dry I'm spittin' dust. I'm a human cinder, no less. Yeah, friends, and I'd like to see the color of the gent's eyes that offers me a drink. It's the first time in my wuthless life I was ever at the head of any list; an', by gravy, that's where I stick."

And stick he did, contrary to all expectations, wagers,

and the law of averages. A half century later, when Preacher Todd had passed, the brothers Poole and Whiskey Gulch were but a memory, and only the church yet stood, an ancient document, yellowed by time, still bore in faded but legible letters the name of Applejack Jim.

There was an interval, however, when his name stood alone as a cash contributor. He headed a list that for several days did not materialize. This was not because the genial citizens of the Gulch were shy or reserved in matters financial. It was a prodigal era. But it was Preacher Todd's move, and they awaited developments.

They were also waiting, with chuckling anticipation, for the reaction of "Steamboat" Sully, a downright person of tremendous influence in Whiskey Gulch.

Steamboat was a vast, bulky individual, hard-featured, hard-fisted, with a bellowing voice and a dominant eye. First a freighter to the Gulch, then an operator of rich claims, he had turned his attention and capital, as the diggings began to fail, to the acquisition of rich grazing lands. Now his herds were swelling in numbers, and the boundaries of his cattle empire were reaching farther east and west along the fertile valley of the John Day.

A species of uncrowned king of the Gulch was Steamboat, a molder of public thought. He led; others followed. It was not his habit to offer an opinion, subject to debate; he spoke; and it was final. When he took note of Preacher Todd his words were received with respect.

"That preacher sharp?" boomed Steamboat, in answer to a discreet inquiry; and dismissed the subject with a wave of the hand. "He don't amount to nothin'. Loco, but harmless."

Thus Preacher Todd, representing a new force in

Whiskey Gulch, faced the inertia born of Steamboat's indifference. Interest was keen enough. Men watched him curiously as he labored. Wages were lost and won on Applejack's constancy. Men were conscious of a sneaking compassion, at sight of Todd's lone figure laboring in the blackened debris. But the list on the sign at the edge of the lot carried no new names.

Preacher Todd, whose eyes were those of a dreamer, also had the jaw of a prize fighter. On an epochal day, near sundown, when Steamboat, surrounded by a group of his cronies, was standing in the dusty thoroughfare hard by the entrance to the Lucky Strike, he cast down his shovel with decision. Men moved aside as he approached. Others, sensing something significant in his bearing, came running from afar. Thus, when he faced Steamboat, he also faced a considerable group of spectators stretching to the right and left.

"Brother Sully," he said quietly, "you are a prominent citizen of this community. I am building a church. How much will you donate to this worthy cause?"

Those who knew Steamboat only by reputation held their breath. But close friends of Steamboat knew that the bulky one, who himself invariably hewed to the line, was favorably impressed by the preacher's straightforward and explicit challenge.

"Reverend," said Steamboat, "I ain't the kind of gent that side-steps anything that's put up to him fair and square. You seem to be playin' a lone hand. I'll tell you what I'll do to back yore play. Over on East Beech Creek I've lost a bald-faced steer. He's a three-year-old maverick, and he's got my brand on him—Triangle S. Go get him. He's yours. Haze him into the pot."

The crowd guffawed, though the big man had spoken gravely. Their laughter died before the equal gravity of Preacher Todd as he bowed and replied: "Thank you, Brother Sully."

They watched him stride toward a distant livery stable. They saw him emerge presently upon his decrepit horse, which was not a cow pony; and a borrowed rope was looped clumsily over the pommel of the saddle.

This was at sundown; and on sundown of the following day curious ones saw Preacher Todd returning up the main street of the Gulch. He sat the saddle drunkenly, a frail, hunched figure, shoulders sagging like one who rides on the outer threshold of exhaustion. His horse, streaked with dust and sweat, stumbled as he walked.

A gathering group of spectators at the entrance of the Lucky Strike saw him turn aside into the livery stable. He emerged presently, on foot, and proceeded slowly up the street to the vacant lot, head bowed, looking neither to the right nor the left. He halted before the sign and wrote upon it. Thereafter he seated himself heavily on a near-by stone and with a gesture of weariness buried his face in his hands.

Curious ones drew near to read what he had written. In a somewhat wavering hand a new line had appeared beneath the name of Applejack Jim:

Steamboat Sully $25

They hastened to the Lucky Strike, where Steamboat was roaring at the bar, in stentorian tones, on some political issue of the day. When informed of what was to be read on the sign without, he set down his empty glass, wiped his mouth with the back of a huge and hairy hand, and went out to investigate. There was a general exodus from the place as genial citizens fell in at his heels.

Steamboat read the wavering line. Then he turned and glared down at the huddled figure of Preacher Todd.

"Reverend," he demanded, pointing with a blunt forefinger, "what's this mean?"

The preacher lowered his hands and looked about him at the attentive circle, then up at the towering Steamboat. His face was pale and drawn beneath the grime; but his eyes were steadfast.

"It means," he said slowly, "that I found your bald-faced steer. I brought him in. I sold him to Ham Nelson for twenty-five dollars."

"You found my steer!" exploded Steamboat. "Well, I'm a son of a gun! Where?"

"A long ways away," said Preacher Todd. "Beyond Saddle Mountain."

That was indeed far away, as each spectator knew.

"When did you find the critter? How'd you fetch him in?"

"I've been riding since last night," explained Preacher Todd. "I found him at daylight this morning. In a kind of a swale. In some willows. I chased him for several hours over a very desolate region. He was exceedingly—fleet of foot. Finally I caught him, in a corner of a high cliff, and got my rope over his horns.

"I am inexperienced in these matters." He spoke in self-deprecatory fashion and flushed a little beneath the sweat and grime. "After the rope was on his horns I didn't know what to do next. He pulled the horse down twice. He was a very robust animal and seemed—er—somewhat hysterical.

So I loosened the rope on the pommel, thinking that perhaps I could manage him better, and he immediately charged away and dragged me from the saddle.

"But I hung on." He spoke with pride. "I abandoned the horse and stayed with the steer. Due to the fact that the animal was weary, no doubt, I kept on my feet, though he ran very fast and cunningly dragged me through numerous thickets of chaparral and sagebrush. Finally he plunged into a grove of small pine trees, where he lay down, with his tongue hanging out. So I tied him with the rope and went back for the horse.

"When I returned again the animal had evidently recovered from his weariness somewhat, but lay in a kind of stupor. I was not deceived and knew he would attempt to escape as soon as he regained his feet. So I placed a half hitch about his nose. This curbed his enthusiasm, and after several futile charges he became quite docile. He lay down several times on the way to town, and I was forced to prod him sharply to make him move.

"And that's all there was to it," he ended proudly. "It was quite an undertaking, but I brought him in."

A momentary silence greeted this narrative. Steamboat stood, glaring, his great feet planted, thumbs hooked in his belt. Other hard-bitten men, to his right and left, stirred uneasily, waiting for his reaction.

"Well, I'm a son of a gun," stated Steamboat.

He turned to the sign and from his hip pocket extracted a stub of pencil. His cronies eyed each other almost furtively. Steamboat had publicly designated the preacher as being of no force. Was he now, enraged in that the preacher had turned the tables against him, about to strike his name from the list?

Stooping, Steamboat wrote briefly. He stood aside, and the crowd surged in to see what he had written. There was a murmur of amazement when it was noted that he had merely added a cipher to the amount following his name. The last line on the list now read:

Steamboat Sully $250

"Gents," said Steamboat, waving a hamlike hand, "I've raised my ante. I never thought he could find my steer, and if he found him, he couldn't bring him in. But for twenty-four hours, and him green and unbroke that-a-way, he's been in the saddle, up in them blistering, blasted pinnacles. He found that bald-faced maverick, hazed him to a standstill, and brought him in.

"I'm reneging on what I said the other day." Steamboat glared around the circle. "I don't know much about religion, but they's something behind him. He's right. He's playing an onbeatable game. Any gent that figgers likewise can step up and affix his John Henry on the dotted line, together with whatever amount his stack of chips will stand. Any citizen that feels a little backward can ponder over this undernourished preacher sharp, clingin' to the end of a rope whilst a wild-eyed maverick drags him through the chaparral and sagebrush and acrost the rimrock, but trustin' to the Lord and hangin' on. Gents, how about it?"

Being men of action, the crowd surged forward. They milled about the sign, and the list lengthened with scrawled signatures. When the pledged amounts were totaled it was found to be well up in four figures; and the first church of Whiskey Gulch was assured.

It is recorded that when the dedication ceremonies were

held in the completed structure a great crowd turned out, representing all social strata of the roaring metropolis. Preacher Todd was in the pulpit, and the light from many candles shone on the grave, upturned faces of bearded men. The Poole brothers were there, and Applejack Jim; and in the triumphant anthem that opened the services the bellowing voice of Steamboat Sully led all the rest.

CHAPTER XXVIII

Power Plus

IN THE HARDHEADED engineering world the beauty of the Cascades' peaks and snow fields is secondary to a more practical fact: the range is one of the globe's greatest single sources of hydroelectric power.

This power becomes available in a natural cycle as unvarying as sunrise and sunset. The heaviest snowfall of the continent each winter blankets the crest of the barrier. It melts each summer, producing countless billions of tons of water resting uneasily a half mile to a mile above sea level. Sudden release of this flood would scour the Pacific slope in an annual calamity. Instead it is held back by the protective forest, so that innumerable trickles below the snow fields become brooks meandering through the timber; the brooks join and become robust streams, and the streams merge at last into rivers which empty north and south into the Columbia near the middle of the range, westward into Gray's Harbor and north to Puget Sound from the northern section.

More than one third of the nation's hydroelectrical power is represented by this annual runoff. The Deschutes

River alone, which falls three thousand feet in a hundred miles—enough to permit the construction of sixteen consecutive dams, each higher than Niagara—is capable of producing an estimated 1,000,000 horsepower.

Long before the huge Bonneville and Grand Coulee dams spanned the Columbia the states of Oregon and Washington, within whose borders the Cascades is almost wholly contained, had reaped the benefit of this natural resource. In developed water power per capita and in per capita use, the two states led the nation. The cost for household use was also the lowest in the nation: 2.47 cents per kilowatt hour, or slightly more than half the United States average of 4.07 cents per kilowatt hour. More than 92 per cent of all city and suburban residents and 53½ per cent of the farms were using this power, as compared to 85 per cent of the non-farm population and 19½ per cent of the farmers of the nation. The city of Tacoma has long had the lowest rate among cities of the country. More electric kitchen ranges are used in Portland, population 400,000, than in New York City, whose population is approximately twenty times greater.

The construction of the Bonneville and the incredibly huge Grand Coulee dams—the latter the world's largest man-made structure—would have produced a surplus of power far beyond the needs of the two states except for the coincident outbreak of World War II and the resultant heavy if temporary power demand of war industries. The withdrawal of that emergency demand will again reopen the dormant feud between advocates of federally owned and privately owned utilities.

The impending showdown over the question, "Whose

power surplus?" should wring a chuckle from the aging Wise Ones of the peaks. To them it must seem strangely like observing men come upon a vast treasure and immediately begin to wrangle over whether the pearls, diamonds, and pieces of eight should be carried away in the right hand or the left. Nevertheless it will be a head-on collision between opposing theories, a proving ground where much of the future economy of the nation may be decided.

The lines of battle are clearly marked. The public power crusaders assert that the output of Bonneville and Grand Coulee is a natural resource which belongs to the people and can properly be administered and distributed to the people in the form of "cheap power" only by a non-profit federal agency. If the private utilities obstruct this holy mission they must be slaughtered, hip and thigh.

Defenders of the privately owned utilities, equally belligerent, insist that the bulk of the cost of these monumental dams has been charged to other and sometimes non-existent "public benefits," such as navigation, flood control, and a vast irrigation system not yet beyond the blueprint stage. Since "the people" must pay for the dams under whatever bookkeeping guise, they assert, from what magician's hat will the rabbit called "cheap power" emerge? Particularly since the current administrative costs of the federal agency in control of Bonneville and Grand Coulee are already larger than the combined administrative costs of *all* privately owned utilities of the Northwest.

The questions are still to be decided. Whatever the outcome, as the Watchers know, the snow will continue to fall and melt each season along the high sky line, and the Columbia will roll on to the sea as usual. To the spectator winging toward the Cascades, high above Grand Coulee, "man's mightiest work" is a mere ripple in the ribbonlike river, which itself is soon shouldered from view by the massive ramparts of the mountains.

On that same note—appropriately—the inventory of the Cascades rounds out, the final and best perspective is glimpsed from the sky.

Higher than the airliners usually travel above the range, from a point in space loftier than Rainier and approximately above the Columbia gorge, the aviator looks down at the sprawling bulk of the last continental barrier. He is facing west, and behind him the high plateau extends like a tawny sea eastward. Directly ahead is a different world, almost entirely green, bordered by the far-off glint of the Pacific. The dividing wall is directly below: a two-hundred-mile segment of the range which stretches north and south, and dips down unbroken another hundred and fifty miles beyond each of the misty horizons. More than half the range's mighty peaks are in view, from Rainier's rounded bulk in the north to the triple spires of the Three Sisters, bold against the southern rim; and between are many lesser crags, like fragments of surf cresting a mighty swell in a green, motionless sea.

The static panorama brings into focus the place occupied by the Cascades both in the continental picture and in its relation to the Pacific slope. The great barrier divides and protects, and its two dominant functions are utility and beauty. Perhaps nowhere on the globe are men more dependent upon a single source for their material, aesthetic, and recreational needs.

The size of the outspread vista is literally symbolic. Just

as the individual peaks highlighted on this broad canvas affirm by suggestion the vastness of the distances between, so the accumulated findings of three generations of exploration, which has been carried out like a many-pronged assault on an isolated but enormous citadel, merely call attention to those areas and categories still marked "potential," "undeveloped," and "unknown." This in itself is not the least of the beckoning and challenging facets of the multi-jeweled range.